Who's Pulling Your Strings?

(Behavior in the misinformation age)

John Cleverly

1st Edition

Author's Partner in Publishing Ltd.

WHO'S PULLING YOUR STRINGS?
Behavior in the Misinformation Age
By: John Cleverly

Published by: Author's Partner in Publishing Ltd
Suite 551 - 800
15355 - 24th Avenue
White Rock, British Columbia
Canada V4A 2H9

Canadian Cataloguing in Publication Data
Cleverly, John
Who's pulling your strings?: behavior in the misinformation age

1st Ed. Includes bibliographical references

ISBN 0-9680808-0-4
1. Social control. 2. Socialization. I. Title.
BF632.5.C54 1996 303.3 C96-900428-1

Dedication

This book is dedicated to all those willing and able to reach a certain level of objective awareness. For those whose blood pressure remains constant while reading this book, there will be a recognition of the enemy that fetters the mind, and warps the judgement.

Table of Contents

FOREWORD

The human mind is a bastion of bias and rejection, stimulated and fed by experience and the five senses. It reaches conclusions by association and cross-referencing of ideas. Our earliest childhood teachings, accepted unconditionally from the adult, form the foundation for all subsequent thinking, for - whether the message is spoken, written or given by example - it is the message we get that powers the mind and determines our future. We've read much about the power of suggestion, and yet we do not examine and purge our own programming of damaging nonsense. For instance, the prevailing doomsday perception of cancer is probably the insurmountable obstacle to a cure. Death becomes a self-activating prophesy. And a child taught the concept of a compassionate and all-seeing god, attributes future fortuitous happenings as the work of that god.

The mind develops as a network of ideas relying on the concepts of early instilled suggestions - that can be no more than extremely damaging opinions - upon which we build the foundation of our mind-set. An opinion inculcated as a truth becomes an integral part of our built-up psyche that henceforth rejects new and conflicting ideas as being unacceptable.

Religion is a part of the social fabric of most countries around the world, but the argument that religions do more good than harm is no longer valid in an open arena of invasive communication, competition and violence. In a world of evolutionary change, the concept of an all powerful protective God has gone from a therapeutic idea within the confines of a tribe, through a period of tyrannical authority that burned disbelievers at the stake, to the present continual warring, and annihilating of whole societies.

We are all, without exception, behaviorally programmed. We are all, to a greater or lesser degree, behaviorally manipulated. And we are all, to some extent, mind-poisoned and controlled by early suggestion and example. But perhaps more revealing is the fact that we all, whether consciously or unconsciously, try to manipulate others to our way of thinking. Because behavioral programming can effectively imprint in a single moment or sentence, even a sibling cannot have comprehensive knowledge of the turning points in his brother's programming, though he himself may have played a major role in that programming. And yet, without such knowledge, society expects to understand the rationale behind a man's misanthropic behavior, and attribute incomprehensible behavior to insanity or criminality, rather than programming.

No two people consistently experience the same programming. The human brain has more than one hundred billion neurons, and with more than a thousand synapses per neuron, activity adds up to about one hundred trillion electro-chemical discharges within the brain. Even when we discount the fact that much of our sensory stimulation and response is identically duplicated, the possible permutation of ideas and experience that make up the range of programmed behavioral differences in people is truly astronomical.

In the following writing, the villains are mental viruses; ideas that make victims out of the unsuspecting. There is no blame, but only the tragedy of generations of programmed aberrational behavior. We'll reflect on human life as it has evolved, and aspire to objectivity in a realistic assessment of what we are, and where we are. We'll attempt to provide answers and explanations for those who seek purpose, hope and direction in their lives as they live it, rather than seeking salvation after death.

The detrimental effects of certain aspects of religious suggestion is a subject too long ignored by both writers and publishers - largely because of a preconceived “no win” scenario. Religion is regarded as an unassailable rampart, a sacred and non-profitable ground. This book is written for no other reason than to break that silence - which is a tacit agreement to leave well alone - and prove damage, prove alienation from reality, and prove the seeding of hate that makes its victims vulnerable to mindless behavior. On the fiftieth anniversary of V.E. day, it is time we realized the truth, and stopped blaming the German people for acts that each and every one of us could have committed. It is time we became aware of the reasons why the human condition is fraught with continual strife and turmoil. It is time we became aware of what causes the killings.

The omission of one comma or dash can frustrate access into an electronic computer. With impartiality, we can view these wonderful machines and say “garbage in, garbage out.” In other words, we can acknowledge that computers are no more accurate than the data fed into them by the programers. But because human minds are the biased products of programming within the biological computers called brains, programmed with manipulative propaganda, fears, hypocrisy, and mythological beliefs passed down from an early evolutionary period, we cannot recognize the garbage that we, in good faith, perpetuate in the development of our children and our children's children.

Furthermore, because our biological computers are confused by emotional and judgmental interpretation, perceiving other dimensions such as love and hate, sadness, joyousness, jealousy, good and evil, we cannot see ourselves as the walking, talking, confrontational aggressors that we really are, in truth more volatile, more dangerous, and less accurate than our more limited but unbiased electronic brain children.

We cannot survive without associating ideas, but even this essential process can have both positive and negative impact on our behavior. Mental association enhances perception and interpretation, but it can also program damaging generalization. For instance, a black man deeply wronged by a white man henceforth distrusts all white men. Of course, the reverse can also be true.

The strength and development of mankind is in the accumulated knowledge passed down from preceding generations, but our weaknesses - our violence, confusions, unfounded beliefs and fears - are derived from the same source. As a species, our degree of developed knowledge creates insecurity, for where imagination is as strong, and conflicts with truth, partial awareness is a pit of dreadful possibilities. We look for messages of hope, and, in the majority, embrace religions and unsubstantiated opinions. But only the messages of truth have been responsible for whatever progress we have made as a species.

There is a popular misconception, endorsed by every religious establishment, that in order to teach our children acceptable social behavior - honesty, kindness, forgiveness, law-abiding accord etc - we must give them the benefit of spiritual teaching. Religions around the world diplomatically and opportunistically embrace these indisputable values, but spiritual teaching (which is synonymous with the concept of a soul or a separate spirit capable of traveling after the death of its earthly host) is in no way related to acceptable social behavior. The concept of hell instills fear of a dreadful reckoning after life, and gives young children frightening nightmares. Other fears arise from parental accounts of devils and demanding gods. Children become paranoid and deeply confused because they are mentally incarcerated in a cage of viral ideas that constitute mental garbage which needs to be sifted and purged from the truths that have raised us above the animals.

Propaganda isn't just the tool of dictators and fascist governments seeking to control human beliefs and behavior. Manipulative propaganda is hypocrisy magnified, and we are all programmed to use hypocrisy and manipulative behavior. Even a child's tantrum for a chocolate bar is learned manipulative behavior.

This book is more observational than speculative, and as such cannot be called philosophical. It is about observed and researched causes and effects of human behavior. It attempts to present a capsulated account of the damaging effect of misinformation gleaned through mankind's evolutionary journey. For convenience sake, the generic term "man" is sometimes used to mean the human race, but in no way denigrates the female of the species.

Some publishers, and even a prominent politician, have already privately denounced this book as being unfit for publication on the grounds that while perhaps being factually correct, it is politically unacceptable, especially on the American scene. This politician even suggested it should and would be banned. It is this type of programmed rejection that makes the publishing of this book an imperative. America takes an inordinate pride in having individual freedom; freedom of speech, freedom of movement, and freedom to choose one's occupation within the parameters of opportunity and qualification. It also take pride in its religious freedom, but the individual seldom changes his birth religion Religious freedom is really the legislated tolerance provided by the State for different sects and denominations to co-exist side by side, a legislated condition that sometimes prevents bloodshed, but never acrimony.

Few of us choose our religion. Most of us are programmed from birth to a particular religion, and in the programming we unwittingly lose a vital part of our mental freedom to accept uncompromising truth without first trying to reconcile it with previously programmed opinion.

This other "freedom in thought" is to this day a virtually unknown freedom in a world that has evolved under the yoke of fear, ignorance and superstition. Each succeeding generation has blindly embraced the religious doctrine of good versus evil; a doctrine built on the fear of the unknown. A doctrine that seeks answers in metaphysical teachings, and through mythological beliefs, all being legacies of a long redundant past.

Our children have never been taught, and are therefore unaware, that the assimilation of a new and somewhat comforting, but erroneous belief - when taught as truth - can deprive them of an area of free reasoning, and - without awareness of the loss - they remain handicapped against the ability to think freely. It is not just freedom for thought without the obstacle of mental reconciliation, but freedom from being manipulated by a viral idea that entices its victims into a life-lasting cocoon of fantasy; a haven from the vicissitudes of life by way of an imaginary alliance with an all-powerful savior, an idea that in reality weakens self-reliance and worldly purpose.

The victims of this form of mental incarceration are legion. They are unaware of being deprived or handicapped, and continue to think themselves the masters and instigators of their own thoughts and direction. In truth, the human animal is so susceptible, so vulnerable to this insidious form of suggestion, that he often wastes a lifetime performing repetitively to a viral idea like a mindless marionette.

Viral ideas that incarcerate the mind can induce radical changes in behavior. The behavioral profile of a conscientious conformist desperately seeking to perform within the restrictive parameters of a mental cage might be as follows: Repetitive behavior that becomes ritualistic addiction, masochistic renunciation of all pleasurable pursuits, and unconscious withdrawal from the threat of opposing ideas that could cause deviation or doubt, which in turn often leads to a form of voluntary physical incarceration. Without wishing to be unkind, monks and nuns exemplify these behavioral patterns. Before entering their isolated islands of dedicated worship there is still some hope for rehabilitation, but two months inside, surrounded by their peers of a similar affliction, and their chance of ever dying outside its "protective" walls is greatly reduced.

On the other hand, a person similarly programmed, but with later exposure to conflicting ideas that cause inner feelings of doubt and unresolved direction, could have quite a different behavioral profile: Depending on the strength and combination of programming, he might be crippled with indecision, and frustrated with an inner fury, directing his explosive temperament, not within himself, which could be self-destructive, but toward others whom he may perceive as being negative factors in his problem. He may seek the confirmation of others with similar programming, and even develop an eloquence of expression to support his revolving arguments. He may in fact be another Hitler, and succeed in bursting out of his programmed mode with the violence of an erupting volcano.

Those victims who have been so programmed are psychological prisoners, no less intelligent, no more and no less righteous, but never-the-less somewhat less responsible for their predictable and arbitrary rejection of the ideas incorporated in this book. Still further, because there are hundreds of associated ideas flowing through this book, all coming from a single source of programming and research - and all written from a single expertise of expression - even the most liberal minded reader will not condone or agree with every idea, for no two people have the same mind print or perspective. However, for all readers who persevere, this book will heighten an awareness of their vulnerability, and provide a more analytical view of themselves.

CHAPTER 1

Aberrational Behavior From Manipulative Propaganda

The church-goer sitting in the pew, listening to the sermon from the pulpit, standing to sing hymns, and putting a dollar or two on the collection plate, certainly doesn't see himself as being manipulated, or as a victim of harmful programming. Quite the contrary, he sees himself as one secure in worship of a praise-worthy God. However, any form of genuflection, such as closing the eyes, bowing the head, kneeling, crossing oneself, singing praises or praying, or even the act of making a donation on a plate - that never starts off empty - is a ritualistic response to a suggestion, a coercive and manipulative programming.

Even most non-believers believe that religion is an innocuous, comfort-giving pursuit of laudable teachings, and so it is, when practiced in a closed society of harmoniously programmed thinkers. However, today we are no longer insulated in small isolated communities. We live in a world community of diverse thinkers, with eleven main competing religions, and because each promulgates only their own unique God, there are proprietary but opposing religious convictions, some with a fanatical devoutness that easily turns to violence.

Universal belief in a supreme God would in itself be harmless and perhaps be beneficial to a sense of well-being. Such a general belief would not repudiate the God of other religions, and might even contain an element of truth. However, an instilled belief - that began as a human cult, and is by no means universal - in a unique, personal God, who created the universe, is a man-made concept that denies and challenges the authenticity of all other religions, and becomes a permanently recurring reason for conflict throughout the world.

We think of Iran as a country of religious fanatics, but America is one of the most religious countries in the world, and has its share of fanatics. Religion is part of its social fabric; a sanctuary for the lonely, a place of song for the musical, a social club for the old and disenfranchised, and a meeting place for the young and amorous. It is the underlying sense of communion with the one true and unique God that is the proven dangerous and destructive belief, because while there is supposedly religious freedom within a country, there certainly isn't religious tolerance throughout the world.

Religion is not just a belief in a God. A dictionary definition of a religion goes as follows - : "a personal set or institutionalized system of religious attitudes, beliefs, and practices." Therefore it is not just differing opinions as to whose God is the true God, but whose method of worship is the correct method, and what attitude of piety should one have toward one's God. All religions re-enforce their support and belief with ritual and genuflection, but in no way is the Christian world about to emulate the exhibitionism of those other "heathen" countries that straddle the globe and have the temerity to compete. All religions assume they have the privilege of communing with a unique and all powerful God, and all take the obvious attributes of good and civilized societies and give credit to their own God as the creator.

Religious teaching not only brainwashes its victims to a particular belief, it also imbues them with a sense of righteousness that makes them feel more worthy, and more deserving. The resulting self-centered superiority creates an attitude of intolerance toward non-believers and those of a different religious persuasion, whose attitude is reciprocal. A sense of righteousness satisfies an ego that craves recognition as being something special, and apart from the common herd. The result is divorce, rift and strife within families, and wars between nations. Religious teaching not only polarizes differences in human relationships, it creates confrontational differences that cannot be reconciled.

Religions are ideas emanating from the mind of man, as are societal standards. Christians psychologically elevate themselves as the ultimate creation, made in the image of their creator, and they thus insinuate themselves into being their God's principal concern, his disciples. They assume the right to speak for their God, espousing his alleged doctrines through human tongue. And some religions are provocative and rabble rousing, and more dangerous than a loaded gun.

We must recognize our worldly religions for what they really are, and for what they do to their followers. Religions originated as a vicarious source of manipulative power and reward for the programmed principals within the religious establishment. They are the legacies left by successful cults. The insidious seeds of manipulative ideas, planted in the human mind by cult leaders, have been nurtured with repetition, ritual, supportive collaboration by like-programmed-thinkers, and - in the West especially - the commercialized motives of the capitalistic system going for its yearly economic Christmas binge, until time and distorted mythology have bestowed the status of a religion.

Religions are mental viruses that invite one to disown one's life; to abrogate personal responsibility. They become mental obsessions that instill fatalism, dependency, and disfunction, the major causes of mass aberrational behavior.

Religions, then, as shall be demonstrated, are far from harmless. They are devious routes to the sub-conscious, bringing forth intolerance and hatred, and rallying political support to kill, pillage and rape, all in the name of righteousness. Religion tunnel-visions the thinking of its followers. And we are not limiting our discussion to such radical cults as the Moonies, though the principle is the same.

The Moonies, ever seeking an instant and malleable congregation, zero in on the adolescent; the young person who has not yet created a strong self-image, who thinks himself to be without worth, and has an overwhelming need to meet his peers and "belong." With low self-esteem, such a person is susceptible to seductive suggestions that mesh with his emotional needs. A friendly environment that flatters the timorous and offers a haven away from demanding parents is probably all the incentive such a young person will need to become a willing participant in the repetitive rituals that will lead to the yielding of "self." The mental prostrations that follow will eventually take over his life, for the unprogrammed individual has a mental void that readily accommodates the strong and appealing dogma of those who would fill it.

David Koresh, who believed himself to be Jesus Christ, headed an apocalyptic cult in Mount Carmel, in Waco, Texas. His cult was one of many around the world where an egomaniacal leader transferred madness to his followers by transferring confused and conflicting opinions. Programming of conflicting opinions can cause madness, or at the very least defective judgement. A relatively poor man can be brainwashed into regularly withholding bread from his family by donating beyond his means to the church, and has no regret for having done so. Indeed, the greater the sacrifice, the greater the feelings of self-righteousness, for we all have a degree of masochism in us.

Religious opinion of what constitutes blasphemy was spoken through the tongue of Iran's Ayotollah Ruhollah Khomeini, who put the black spot on the writer, Salman Rushdie, with a substantial reward for the opportunistic murderer who would come forward to claim it. Conspiring to murder is apparently a divine right for the rulers of Iran. This has created a precedent in the Muslim world, and so, five years later, a feminist writer from Bangladesh, Tamila Nasrin, had a similar death sentence placed on her by the Muslim extremists, for suggesting that the Muslim teachings of the Koran be somewhat relaxed with regard to the limiting of the women's role to housework and child-rearing.

The Reverend Jim Jones, who orchestrated the Jones' Town Massacre, was another charismatic (if insane) leader who gained such control over his parishioners that he literally talked almost a thousand of them into committing suicide. In truth, loving parents killed their children on the instruction of this one man, before killing themselves. Jones was a paranoiac, the victim of devastating aberrational programming. He hated the Bible with an unnatural passion, and frequently spat on it, or used its pages as toilet paper. He distrusted all men, and used only women in the top echelon of his "Christian" movement. But a thousand people allowed this damaged egomaniac to persuade them to murder and commit suicide. History tells us we are, in fact, all susceptible, to some degree, to self-destructive suggestion, and, without this awareness, the information age could make even more of us vulnerable.

We are aware of these few cults largely because they were spawned on American soil within recent living memory, but the history of mankind is pock-marked with the rise and fall of such unsuccessful cults. They are the natural and predictable behavioral patterns of a species programmed by an evolutionary past to seek sanctuary with a savior to ensure survival in a world of bloody predators, a past that entertains death by giving a second chance, a past that condemned the ignorant to a dependency on superstition and myth.

We have trouble accepting the Jewish holocaust because it was within our living memory. We can accept the French Revolution, and the use of the guillotine. We can reconcile ourselves to the idea of the ancient Romans callously throwing Christians to the lions. Succeeding generations have become disassociated by denial and the argument that these were atrocities of a bygone era - when we were more primitive. Yet, in terms of evolutionary time, these happenings were only yesterday. Recorded history has proven us capable of crucifying, torturing, burning dissidents at the stake, or even hacking others to pieces - for merely having had the gall to entertain differing opinions. Evolution has made us accomplished killers, and the only change has been our very recent access to technological advancements that make better means of communication an easier route to confrontation and more efficient killing techniques, in a shrinking world that has become our killing field.

Because of the passing of a generation, we are already forgetting and denying the Jewish holocaust that saw the extermination of six million Jews. Time and nature obliterate the evidence. New generations have no memories of the macabre horrors now hidden in mass graves beneath picnic spots of lush grasses and cool breezes. There are those who would rewrite history, only too willing to forget the infamy of Auschwitz, Belsen, Buchenwald, Dachau, and in fact some three hundred other killing camps spread throughout Germany.

Young neo-Nazis, without experience or memories of the atrocities of war, are again marching the streets of Germany, and are in fact in the process of being brainwashed and re-programmed by such power-hungry manipulators as Zundel. Zundel, today's short and tubby version of Goebbels, the late German propagandist, is operating his propaganda machine out of Canada - a country that appears to have some difficulty in distinguishing the difference between opinionated propaganda, commercialized and distributed wholesale to incite up-rising and violence - in fact insurrection - and the right to freedom of speech and circumspect "religious freedom."

Zundel has been labeled either a liar, a fool, or a hypocrite by those who remember the holocaust, but he may be neither one. He may have been programmed to genuinely believe that the recorded annihilation of six million Jews was a fabrication by the Western Allies to permanently place Germany on the defensive. Zundel certainly doesn't have a franchise on propaganda, but he's intelligent enough to know that he must first discredit the evidence of the holocaust in the minds of the new generation of German youth, before having them rise up against a perceived injustice. And, as in Germany's second attempt for world supremacy, youth must again be programmed in the belief of their superiority and invincibility.

Germany is one of the few countries in the world that restricts citizenship on the basis of the bloodline. The German population has long been programmed to believe that their blood line is superior to that of the rest of the world, in that their work ethic and sense of responsibility is a result of that bloodline. The deprived, and unemployed German youth, inherently arrogant and aggressive, are only too ready to believe both propositions. However, their sense of superiority lies only in their arrogant programming, and not in their bloodline.

It is a frightening scenario for those veterans old enough to have witnessed the happenings of the second world war, and who can testify to the mad rampage of the Nazi regime. The dozens of news reels from all countries, the personal photographs, the ovens and gas chambers, the cramped barracks, the huge piles of prescription glasses and dentures, the personal possessions that were left behind, the pitiful carvings on wooden bunks and walls by men, women and children, now sharing tangled graves, all testify to the horror. There is an abundance of evidence, including the most damning living memories of the survivors. Soon there won't be any survivors, but these memories must be kept alive by inculcating future generations with awareness - not to punish the German people - but to remind the whole of mankind of the insidious effects of mass manipulation by propaganda programming.

As a consequence of Hitler's holocaust, three generations of Germans have had to carry the burden of shame before the entire world. Many elderly Germans, now living abroad, even deny their nationality. Others still glory in their supposed superiority. As for the youth of Germany, they think that by denial they will erase the latest stigma on the Germanic race. But denial is not exoneration, and the stigma is on the whole human race, for - given the programming - each one of us is capable of activating the bestiality that lies dormant within.

Those few who are programmed, against all evidence to the contrary, to disbelieve and teach that the holocaust never happened, are not advocates of free speech, but treacherous advocates of opinion over established truth, the main cause of confused and aberrational behavior. If we allow denial of the most infamous massacre the world has ever seen, if - after only two generations - we allow forgetfulness, we are blinding our descendants to their fallibility. We are again using the programming of opinion to deny reality.

The instigators of the holocaust were victims of other programmed victims dating back to the 1869 teachings of Francis Galton and his writings on hereditary genius, promoting the idea of producing a superior race. There followed years of racial persecution. In 1904 Karl Pearson publicly denounced the high birth rate of the poorer, "less intelligent" as a threat to civilization. A year later the American Eugenics Society proclaimed that the white race, especially those of Nordic background, represented the cream of human developed intelligence. Fifteen years later it went even further, associating low intelligence with criminal behavior. Both Canada and the United States enacted laws that restricted the entry of the Asiatic people into their countries on the grounds that they were undesirable stock. In 1924 eugenicists advocated the sterilization of mentally defective persons. In 1928 Alberta introduced a sterilization bill. In 1931 more than half the States of the USA, Switzerland, Germany, Denmark and Norway followed suit.

When Hitler came to power in 1935, the Nazis resurrected the theories of Karl Pearson with regard the superiority of the Nordic race. And so, generations of programming culminated in the Nazi belief in German racial superiority. Catholicism was the predominant German faith, and became synonymous with that euphoric sense of superiority and righteousness that rallied the German population. "Superiority" became power, and Jews became mere pests, rats who must be exterminated.

Between 1938 and 1940, the Nazis built their first fifteen concentration camps, and commenced the systematic annihilation of the "genetically inferior" Jew. The opportunists seized the chance to get rid of other "social undesirables" such as the homosexuals, the gypsies and the defectives. But those who perpetrated the holocaust were, in a sense, also victims of programming. In order to function we must all be programmed, and only the fortunate who have an undamaged sense of awareness, to alert them to the difference between truth and opinion, will be equipped to resist the manipulation that will denigrate them.

Such wholesale slaughter, as witnessed in the Jewish holocaust, could only have been instigated and enforced by a programmed regime that believed in its superiority and divine right to eliminate the "forces of evil." Hitler, the prime egomaniac and instigator, suffered early personal failures and experiences that warped his judgement and distorted his behavior. His early personal failures drove him to express his hatred, and seek success and recognition through the efforts of others. But while it's one thing to understand how hate propaganda and the trauma of the times emotionalized the perpetrators to participate in such acts, it's quite another to understand how one egomaniac, even one as charismatic and eloquent as Hitler, could surround himself with others of a like mania; to rally enough plurality to regenerate national feelings of superiority, feelings of invincibility, feelings of hatred and blame for the Jews. It's difficult to understand unless we find a common denominator in the backgrounds of those who came together to form the Third Reich.

To find that common denominator, we don't have to dig very deeply. Like all politicians, the nucleus of the Nazi party learned very early to avoid making controversial public declarations, or taking a public stance on any issue that might arouse anger and opposition - at least until they were firmly entrenched within a power structure founded on fear.

The principal architects of the holocaust were: Adolf Hitler, Heinrich Himmler (both obsessed with Lance's theory for the purification of an Aryan race), Reich Marshal Hermann Goering, Doctor Josef Mengele, (the sadistic surgeon who delighted in human experimentation) the diminutive Paul Joseph Goebbels, (the propagandist of the Nazi party), and Julius Streicher, the hate monger who wrote exclusively against the Jews in "Der Stürmer." Then there was Heines, Ernst Roehm, who was a disfigured pervert, and last - because of his teachings and influence on Hitler at an earlier age - Dietrich Eckhart. This nucleus of the Nazi party were reticent to talk about their early religious training, because they needed unanimous support from a country that was not, and is still not, unanimous in its denominational Christian conviction.

In a Christian society, it is perhaps considered too abrasive and inflammatory to gather the following facts in a standard encyclopedia. It points the finger and speaks ill of an accepted religion within our own western civilization. For obvious reasons, the following facts were never brought out, or even mentioned as a causal factor at the Nuremberg war crime trials. Religious prejudice was protected by the derogatory phrase "anti-Semitism." However, it is a recorded fact that the bloodthirsty nucleus, the top echelon of the German third Reich, were all products of early programming in Catholicism, a religion that embraces the concept of the "forces of evil," which - according to Hitler and his cronies - had taken up residence in the Jewish faith. This was the common mania in Germany that was responsible for initiating an organized killing campaign to exterminate their fellow countrymen, the Jews. And not just killing them, but robbing them, raping them, shaving their heads, skinning them to make lamp shades, taking their gold teeth fillings for melting down, and humiliating them with a hatred not afforded the verminous rat.

There are hundreds of books written on Anti-Semitism; books that talk of the psychology of Anti-Semitism in the Nazi party - books that lay blame. But it is not enough to attribute the hatred and bestial behavior to Anti-Semitism. That label fails to explain why. And also it's not enough to restrict the area of hatred to Germany just because on this occasion it happened to erupt in that area. It later erupted in Bosnia, and Rwanda. In truth religious intolerance is world-wide, largely because Catholicism is world-wide, and Anti-Semitism is the rallying cry of the Catholic Religion. This is where the programming of hate for the Jews originated. Ethnic cleansing is a Roman Catholic directive. The world needs to be aware that certain aspects of Catholicism contain dangerous weird ideas.

Hate viruses are ideas that are easily implanted in the human mind, for they feed and grow on every perceived difference. Nourished by coveting and comparison, and nurtured by every conceivable slight, mannerism, accent, or color of skin, they point out the whipping boy for self-failure. When the hate virus is passed to and fro and targeted on one subject, country or religion, it becomes a devastating power to incite and unite "like thinkers" to the violence of a hanging party. The technique is used extensively for this purpose by cult leaders, and those who perpetuate their doctrines in every corner of the world. Beware! For those who listen to hate are destined to become its victims. Hate propagates resentment and loathing, to fill the mind and spread its contagion to anyone who will listen. Because of the more physical violence in the past of the male, hate erupts in fits of sudden, unreasonable violence. In the female, it simmers with spite and deception, in more subtle and life-lasting grudges.

Hitler was a choir boy in a Benedictine monastery, and in later years talked of "going into the church." (Biography of Hitler: by Jaochim C. Sest.) Goebbels came from a very devout Catholic family, taught Catholicism, also had aspirations of becoming a priest, but instead married a Jewess, and later became "The man who created Hitler": by Viktor Reimann. Reich Marshal Hermann Goering was actually introduced into Catholicism by a Jew posing as a Catholic. (Reich Marshal: by Leonard Mosely.) Heinrich Himmler was the son of a very strict Catholic secondary school master. Julius Streicher was raised in a Catholic family of nine children. Both parents frequently expressed hatred for the Jews, and the father, who was also a school master, encouraged five of his children to follow in his footsteps and become teachers. In the classroom, Streicher was not reticent in teaching his version of religious bias for the "spiritual benefit" of his students. He later proved himself to be a depraved sadist who carried a whip in his waistband, and boasted openly of its use.

Deitrich Eckhart, a Catholic, and an early influence on Hitler after the first world war, had been in a mental asylum. Ernst Roehm was a Catholic, a disfigured sadist, with part of his nose shot off, and a homosexual to boot. Heines was another sexual pervert who scoured Germany for suitable bed fellows.

There were others in the party who were not Catholics, but who had been brain-washed by the propaganda. Hess was an Evangelist, a Buchmanite, who deserted the party and fled to England under poorly explained circumstances. Alfred Rosenberg was a philosopher who, like Himmler, had an obsession for Aryan superiority, but who wrote extensively against all religions. He wrote "Myth of the 21st century."

Hitler's closest and most influential companion and confidant, the Reich Marshal Hermann Goering was, as a small child, regularly taken to the Catholic Mass by his beloved godfather, Ritter von Epenstein, a rich and flamboyant bachelor and benefactor to Hermann's entire family. They lived at Mauterndorf, one of Epenstein's castles, and Hermann's father became a cuckold, with von Epenstein regularly sleeping with Hermann's mother and eventually giving her a child.

It is likely that little Hermann was too young to really understand what was going on, because he remained Epenstein's admirer until, at the age of eleven, he paeaned the praises of his hero in a school essay entitled: "The man I admire most in the world." Whereupon his "high" master took him aside to inform him that Ansbach boys do not sing the praises of "Jews." When Goering hotly denied the allegation that Epenstein was a Jew, the master produced a copy of the semi-Gotha, a written record of all the German Jews aspiring to aristocracy. A few hours later the story had spread around the school, and Goering was frog-marched around the grounds with a placard around his neck, "Mein Pate ist ein Jude."

Epenstein allowed the Goering family to stay on at Mauterndorf for a total of fifteen years, and then - at sixty-two years of age - fell in love with a twenty-year-old, whom he married. The elderly Heinrich Goering, a broken man, moved his family out of Mauterndorf castle, and died shortly afterwards, with Hermann, now an officer in uniform, crying like a child at the funeral. As a small child, Herman was in effect literally introduced into the Catholic faith by a Jew posing as a Catholic; the same Jew that gave charity to his family, while seducing his mother and giving her a child.

Hermann Goering, known as "Jolly Hermann," was unstable if not psychotic, often surprising his associates with violent mood swings. "I remember coming away from my first meeting asking myself the question: How had such a worldly, cultivated man got himself mixed up with such a sleazy and murderous gang as the Nazis? I was somewhat chastened shortly afterward when I went to one of his meetings and saw on the platform not the charming art and animal lover I had first encountered, but a ranting, raving anti-Semite mouthing all the shibboleths of the Party, a quivering mass of hate and rancor." (Reich Marshal; by Leonard Mosley)

While the instigators of the holocaust were all Catholics, many of the perpetrators who carried out the atrocities were of different religions, brainwashed by Germany's hate propaganda dating as far back as the Kaiser's day - propaganda later reinforced by the Nazi team: Goebbels, Julius Streicher in his "Der Stürmer," and A. Rosenberg in his daily, "Volkischer Beobachter," and the "Party Organ Review."

But of course religious intolerance is not confined to any particular religion. Adolf Eichmann, personally responsible for thousands of deaths, was a Protestant. Martin Bormann, another infamous participant, was raised as a Lutheran, as was Joachim Von Ribbentrop, who was also a Free Mason before he entered the Nazi party - which disallowed such an affiliation! (This man Ribbentrop. His Life and Times; by Schwarz.)

The Jews have accused Pope Pius XII, who was in office at the time of the holocaust, saying that the centuries of anti-Jewish theological tradition by the Catholic Church was a major cause of the holocaust. But it was Pope Leo XIII who openly declared war on all other religions with the public statement that "equal tolerance of all religions is the same as atheism." (atheism being a dirty word) This lays down a directive for intolerance. This advocates confrontation and banishment.

A repudiation, provisionally titled "Anti-Semitism, the Shoah and the Church," (Shoah being Hebrew for holocaust) based on a document that originally came out of the German and Polish Bishops' conference, has been currently redrafted by Professor Hans Hermann Henrix of the Catholic Theological Institute in Aachen, Germany. However, as such a publicized denial would cause more doubt than belief, it is unlikely that such a document will ever see the light of day. Joaquin Navarro-Valls, a Vatican official, has already distanced the Church, saying that no church authority has sanctioned such a document, and that it does not reflect the official position of the church at this stage.

The Vatican is well aware of the power of suggestion in the controlling of human behavior. Pope John Paul recently asked for forgiveness for the wrongs his religion has inflicted on other religions, and now - fifty years after the holocaust - it is considered politically expedient to quietly change the New Testament to meet the new political awareness. An admission that the church must be more circumspect in controlling a more sophisticated populous with vicarious programming and manipulation.

In September 1995, the Oxford University Press will put out a revised English version of the New Testament that, among other things, removes the accusation that the Jews were responsible for the death of the Savior. It also states that : Children should "heed their parents" rather than obey them. Wives are no longer subject to their husbands, but committed to them. Darkness is no longer to be equated with evil, and that the Lord's Prayer should begin with "Our Father-Mother in Heaven."

To be sure that they cover all the bases, they also delete references to the "right hand of God" to remove any unfavourable connotation to the left-handed.

Paradoxically, the second factor that united the Nazi leaders in common bond was their subsequent hatred of the powerful Catholic church. These common feelings were revealed in a variety of different ways. It was indeed as though each one was trying to break out of an earlier programmed mode. Hitler often spoke in private against the church, while diplomatically avoiding public denouncement. Goebbels, on the other hand, never spoke in private against the church, but on a number of indiscreet occasions publicly denounced it in very positive terms. Rosenberg quite openly advocated the replacement of Christianity with a Germanic pagan religion. Benito Mussolini, Hitler's friend and war ally, who aided and abetted his every deplorable act, also had some early schooling in Catholicism - probably on his mother's side, as his father was later anti-religion - but Mussolini also subsequently fell out with his church and abolished the Roman Catholic youth organizations.

The instigators of the holocaust, those who gave the initial directive, were psychopaths, victims of irrevocable and incompatible programming that distorted their thinking and provided a basis for the atrocities that followed. They had long forgotten and neglected some of the "love thy neighbor" teachings, but they could never forget or subdue an innate hatred against what was perceived as "the forces of evil." And, in acting out their programming, they became the force of evil. Only now, half a century later, under world-wide pressure, has the Vatican recognized the Jewish State.

And there you have the "why!" And there you have, at the very least, a contributing factor that caused the Holocaust, for given the same circumstances and conditions - the directive, the propaganda, the opportunity, the impetus of war-hate searching for a target, the re-enforcement of colleagues with like-programming, the high level of stress, and mass hysteria - and any one of us might follow a hate directive rather than be out of step with the perceived majority. But that is by no means the end of the story.

The long time "persecution of the Jews" throughout the world has elevated the Jewish faith to the special status of having been the one religion to be sought out and victimized throughout their history by other religions. The reason Jewish history is fraught with abuse, is because from the time of the diaspora, the scattering of the Jews after the Babylonian exile, until 1947, when the United Nations saw fit to partition Palestine into separate Jewish and Arab states, the Jews were literally without a country, roaming the world to intrude on other religions with their own particular brand of religious ritual and dogma.

In the last three decades, archaeologists have found solid evidence (writings, twin altars with offerings, and figurines) that indicates the Israelites of the old world were indeed into cult worship of Yahweh and Asherah, a god and goddess; this was again attributing human sexuality to their gods. But time has changed history and the belief.

Indeed, after two thousand years of roaming, multiplying, and dispersing into the far reaching corners of the world, there are no geographical barriers to the feelings of antipathy toward the Jews. Even those countries that were over-run by the Germans - Poland, Czechoslovakia, Hungary, France, etc, (countries with a devout Christian component) - regarded their Jewish population as intolerable deviants who made a mockery of their own established beliefs. It was a contradiction to a conviction that went to the heart of their psyche, and violence is more often than not the result of indiscreet programming of opinion over opinion.

The Sikhs today are in much the same position as the Jews of two thousand years ago. Without a country of their own, they are going forth to settle in any country that will have them. They are building their temples, and jealously guarding their religion and their culture. As an acquaintance remarked: "I'm no bigot. They can't help their color. But why do they have to wear those stupid turbans? If they want to be Canadians or Americans, why don't they adapt to our way of life? And this business of carrying knives because of their religion is just bloody silly. The whole friggin' bunch need locking up in my opinion!" More than one has said, "prejudice is opinion without judgement." : Voltaire and

Francois Marie Arouet. We could say prejudice is opinion without truth.

Since the Third Reich made its case for the purification of an Arian race, the world has seemingly rushed into producing multi-racial conglomerates to prove them wrong. If we project our present course through the next few centuries there will be no racial differences. Today, every developed country is in the process of becoming a melting pot for the people of the third world, who are seeking to elevate their economic base. Only our religious differences will survive over the years to be cause for future conflict, because we perpetuate our programming in our young, and in the "taking of sides."

Religious freedom is politically expedient in any country of diverse beliefs. Government tolerance of conflicting religions, under a "religious freedom" policy, allows for a less turbulent control, but opinionated differences still surface in violence within these tolerance zones. Religious opinion is creating violence and murder in the name of righteousness around the abortion clinics. In fact, religious opinion is causing mayhem in practically every corner of the present-day world. The only alternative to religious freedom and tolerance is no religion, a tack prematurely used by the defunct Soviet Union, but without any attempt at reprogramming the populace to a secular substitute.

A clever leader takes advantage of preconceived ideas that are predominant within his domain, for those with preconceived ideas are readily susceptible to anything that reinforces them. Sadam Hussein realized that Iraq, which is a Moslem country, could therefore easily become unified in an alliance with the rest of the Arab Moslem world. He was badly in need of allies against the Americans, and so he assumed a fervent religious posture, and pointed his finger at Israel as the intruder and usurper of the "faith." This clever move, and his subsequent bombing of Israel, were designed to unite the Arabs, already technically at war with Israel. Unfortunately for him, the entire world had been apprised of his motives by a system of satellite communication here-to-fore unheard of. Similarly, the Nazi motive for the holocaust has been attributed to their wanting a scapegoat and a diversion against a losing war and a failing morale, but while plausible, that alone does not explain its early implementation, even before the war, and the ready mass acceptance of such a policy.

Opinions differ with perspective, and this is a major cause of war. World leaders view problems from their own narrow perspective, each striving for political and allied advantage. The technologically advanced West viewed Sadam Hussein as a wealthy customer for their technologically advanced armaments, and - pursuing the profit motive - sold him some forty-odd billions of dollars worth of hi-tech killing potential. Hussein saw the transactions as proof of his favoured alliance with the Superpowers, and from it derived a false sense of security. After sounding out his American ambassadress and receiving the ambiguous reply that "America had no interest in interfering in the internal affairs of the Gulf countries," - Hussein was encouraged to invade Kuwait.

The West immediately saw the move as a threat to a major source of oil, and went in to destroy Hussein's war potential. Now, since the culmination of the Gulf war and the continued destruction of Hussein's armoury, the West has continued to sell more than thirty billion dollars worth of offensive technology to other countries around the Gulf. And so, with conflicting perspectives, opinions, and self-interests, we have guaranteed continued unrest and a fool-proof formula for more war.

President Bush was of the opinion that the Iraqi people, having been subjected to adversity, deprivation and defeat by Hussein, would post-war oust him from office. However, mob psychology dictates that adversity is the rallying signal for the closing of ranks around a leader. It happened in Britain during the last world war, when the people rallied around Churchill. It is the legacy of the "sabre tooth tiger syndrome" when the tribe had to collectively kill the beast to prevent piece meal decimation of their numbers. However, without further threat from America, the hardships imposed by world embargoes will eventually drive Hussein from power.

Meanwhile, the Arab world in general is changing its perspective on America, which is losing its status as the powerful arbiter in maintaining world peace. There are already rumblings of discontent at being under the shadow of a super-power that might not always be the "benign" unambitious arbitrator.

In South Africa, Nelson Mandella must do a major job of re-programming and educating if he is to be successful in bringing the blacks and whites together. The lies, the forceful eviction at gun-point of natives from their home-lands, and the subsequent selling off the land to white settlers at a third of the value is still within living memory. The bullying tactics that followed, in order to retain possession of those lands, will take a lot of legal litigation to avoid eventual bloodshed. Wrongs need to be righted, and must be seen to be righted, before blacks and whites can settle in harmony. The relationship between the tiny white component of the population and the intimidating uneducated black majority was analogous to a very small lion tamer in a large den of lions. It was a case of either attempting complete suppression or separation. The result was apartheid, with an intimidating show of superior organization, and wealth.

Today, the world is baffled by the so-called ethnic-cleansing; the cruelty and killings that are being perpetrated in Bosnia-Herzegovina by people who, until the break-up of the Soviet Union, had evolved into living cheek by jowl in a neighborly but uneasy truce. In his very readable and informative book, "Seasons in Hell," Vulliamy explains that what is going on now is a resurrection (after years of Soviet imposed atheism) of a tenth century struggle between Charlemagne's Roman Catholic Frankish empire, (now the Croatians) and the Orthodox Byzantine emperors, (now the Serbs) to re-establish borders that were won by Croatia's King Tomislav's expansion in 924 A.D. At that time the Croatians held territory for three years, stretching from Istria in the West, all the way to the existing Hungarian border, and as far east as the river Drina. The old map was apparently "dug up" by Croatian dissidents hiding in South America at the time of the dissolution of the Soviet Empire.

Now, both sides are indiscriminately slaughtering the Slavic Muslims, (direct descendants of the so-called Bogomil heretics, under Great Ban Kulin of the twelfth century, who later embraced the Islam faith) in another "ethnic cleansing" holocaust. Under the guise of a territorial dispute, religion once again instigates a holocaust.

One must read the book to get the full historical background to this turbulent, multi-religion area, and to appreciate why the conquering of territory becomes synonymous with the conquering of one religion by another. However, it must also be remembered that the infamous Croatian Ustasha, rulers of the Nazi puppet state in 1941/45 Yugoslavia, tortured and murdered more than half a million Jews, Muslims and Serbs, and the hatred still lingers on to fuel the present carnage.

Another area of ethnic cleansing in the form of killing and mayhem that is causing great puzzlement around the world is Rwanda, Burundi, and Zaire, all of which came under the jurisdiction of Germany in 1899. After the second world war the area was entrusted to Belgium, and at that time the comparatively rich Catholic Church of French Quebec sent its missionaries to Rwanda. They recognized the more pleasing physical attributes of the some 780,000 Tutsis (about 14% of the total population) as opposed to the more dour and more prolific Hutus tribe, and spent much time measuring nose length and head size to ascertain the superiority of the Tutsis tribe. As a minority, they were elevated to the ruling class until the disenchanted and disenfranchised majority population of Hutus ousted them and took over government.

The Catholic Church then began wooing the Hutus, spending many millions of dollars to convert them to Catholicism, building their first University, and generally trying to enlighten them to the Catholic ideal while still surreptitiously favouring the Tutsis. Eighty percent of the Rwanda population is now Catholic, with a small component of Protestants and Muslims. The rest are mostly Animists, who believe that all material, including inanimate objects, have souls that are separable from matter, and capable of detachment to roam the earth. This is a twisted form of pantheism, a belief in an all pervasive God that gives smaller precedence to man, and would be anathema to those with monotheistic belief.

The implanted "superiority complex" of the Tutsis created rebellious subjects for a Hutus government, that solved the problem by killing them off at the rate of 250,000 in eighteen months. The idea of superiority and the long-standing jealousy erupted in wholesale massacre, which caused a backlash of fear, with the Tutsis eventually striking back in an all-out killing hysteria, to chase millions of their persecutors, the Hutus, into Zaire, where cholera and dysentery continued the death toll.

These tribes who kill so easily, these hordes with but a single obsession, have been so mind-abused by reciprocal, re-enforcing, and self-righteous dogma, that they are even jealous of sharing a common religion with those they think are of an inferior race. They hate transgressors or disbelievers with a vicious passion, and see each other as usurpers that must be purged out by "ethnic cleansing."

In such areas of conflict among tribes of differing religious beliefs, where aberrational behavior and killings have gone on for thousands of years, no one opinionated side is about to change, and accept blame - if there is blame - for each side sees itself as being a victim of the opposing evil party, and never as a victim of its own programming.

And now, as recently as 1994, two so-called intellectuals, the recently deceased Richard Hernstein and Charles Murray, perpetuated the damaging programming of the past century by writing a best seller - some eight hundred and fifty pages - entitled the "Bell Curve." Addictive beliefs create "truths" in the eyes of the programmed beholders, and the moments of revelation created by such giants as Copernicus, Galileo, and Darwin, are either discounted or twisted to suit other concepts. It was Darwin's cousin, Francis Galton, who took Darwin's work and condensed his findings into a repudiation of the worth of the "lower classes." We fail to learn from such evidence as our anthropological research, the holocaust, or the unvarnished true interpretation of the Dead Sea Scrolls, because we wish to reinforce our preconceived concepts.

Nobody disputes that selective breeding with selective programming would result in an improved human species, but selective breeding alone with the wrong programming could result in another killing hysteria. Though we would all like to believe in our inherent superiority, the reason we are not the savages of this world is the lucky consequence of not being isolated from birth among other savages. Without detracting from the achievers, labeled as geniuses, let us acknowledge that they come from every walk of life, every level of society, and every religion. Let us further acknowledge that the breakthroughs that we have attributed to genius have inevitably been the result of either serendipitous exposure - or the purposeful seeking of further exposure through research - together with the association of ideas gleaned through previous experience. i.e., one truth leading to another.

We program superiority - whether it be in a mythical religious knowledge, or a so-called superior bloodline - and the result is aggression and the desire to dominate. Program inferiority and we get subservience, incompetence, and further aberrational behavior. The balance is competence in realizing that our level of knowledge is badly biased, easily unbalanced, and not comprehensive. Opinion becomes fact in the minds of the programmed. However, any thinking man can see the folly in allowing a religion with its subjective bias into the political arena of a country. However, it would be extremely naive not to realize that religion permeates and influences a majority of households throughout the world. Stronger than any fascist government with its perhaps thousands of informers, the Vatican City with its sensitive antennae, has millions of unwitting informers parading through the confessional box every day.

Disasters like the bombing of the New York Trade Center, the more recent bombing in Oklahoma City, the gassing of Japanese citizens by the Supreme Truth Cult (or the so-called Doomsday Cult), and the assassinations of politicians like Rabin, are the direct results of confused religious aggression. They are the forerunners of a new trend in the aberrational behavior of religious fanaticism.

It would be worthwhile considering further whether indeed there is blame for aberrational behaviour, for there is no such thing as an evil force. There are no evil men, or evil anything. There is only harmful aberrational programming that produces what we interpret as evil. Our conscience is not some innate form of decency that surfaces to place parameters on undesirable behavior. A pricked conscience is merely programming in conflict. Our conscience does not just rise on occasion to pre-empt our programming. Our programming is our conscience, whether compassionate and conforming, or contemptuous and cruel.

There are men who have been programmed to evil or, more accurately, programmed to harmful anti-social consequences. This is more than semantics, and is expounded upon in another chapter entitled "The programming of ethics, morals, and other desirable parameters to human behavior."

—Viral ideas become an integral part of the human psyche, an irrevocable blue-print for future behavior. The human animal is so vulnerable to an appealing idea that he becomes miserable and defeated unless he can conform to its directive, even to the point of self-mutilation or death. In different parts of the world the concept of beauty varies, demanding elongated necks, small - deformed - feet, fat calves, round eyes, circumcised penises, pointed teeth, stretched lips, stretched ear lobes, extraordinary long fingernails that make every ablutionary act a health hazard, tattooed skin, painted faces, and even squeezed, deformed skulls. In the western world, enormous breasts and small straight noses demand a high medical fee. Both the sophisticated and the simplistic demonstrate their desire to be noticed and admired, distancing themselves from the unadorned monkey-like production of the womb. With the programming of the young, these "fashions" become a mandate, for the physical image must equate with the mental image within the mind. It is precisely because we need to be programmed in order to function as living entities, that we so readily embrace ritual, or repetitive action, the easiest and least painful directive of all programming. (Unless, of course, the ritual involves human sacrifice.)

CHAPTER 2

Does Aberrational Programming Absolve Blame?

If we are to accept the proposition that early programming, and/or chemical imbalances, are the determining factors of later behavior, then we must accept the proposition that the onus or responsibility for anti-social and inappropriate aggressive behavior would rest with the original programer - which could go back generations - but certainly not with the individual programmed. The perpetrators of a religious purge are as much victims of their programming as are the victims of their persecution. Hatred and violence emanating from like-thinkers have the contagion of the attacking animal pack. Reaction of this sort is supportive programming in action. We might argue that self-discipline and moral integrity should have come forth to prevent any given individual from participating in the holocaust, but of course the prejudices of early hate programming superseded those desirable traits, just as any computer is incapable of going outside of its programmed curriculum.

There are of course many reasons for aberrational behavior, and many forms and levels of anti-social behavior, ranging from the depravity of serial sex murderers to petty theft, or embezzlement within a social service. The fact that society would collapse into anarchy without individual accountability, would indicate that we would be more effective if we addressed the motivational causes of aberrational behavior rather than measuring and acting upon the emotional effects of its brutality. This is a common argument for the mitigation of blame, and the converting of prisons to correctional institutions, with imposed sentences lasting for only the duration of the cure.

Let us pretend for a moment that we're jurors in the Homolka murder trial: Karla has just finished testifying how she and her husband, Paul, raped, tortured, killed and dismembered one of their victims. Because of our programming of what is acceptable behavior, we are suitably shocked, and search the two young cherubic faces for the evil that must somehow be apparent. Seeing that Karla has slightly hooded eyes, we decide that she was probably the evil instigator. Our human reaction is emotional and speculative. Not seeing a pair of horns, we might think her all the more sinister for looking normal. Photographs of the three young and beautiful victims are passed around the jurors, and our reaction is again an emotional one, and, of course, the result of our own particular programming. Which one is to blame? The more horrific the unfolding story, and the greater the display of senseless, unconscionable cruelty and depravity, the more we focus on effect rather than cause. We think of their behavior as proof positive that they're on the side of the devil, and our sense of righteousness cries out for harsh punishment.

Well, this is our programmed human reaction, and one that has been inculcated in society to bring law and order out of chaos. Even if we could divest ourselves of emotional feelings, it wouldn't make them any less guilty. We cannot sympathize with them, for we can only see brutality without compassion or rationale in their actions. We will never know the earlier convoluted programming that deprived them of conscience, or fear of being found out. During their gory pleasures, they must have felt invincible, and beyond the reach of the law.

Their defense is not based on insanity, but they are surely the victims of their own programming. On the evidence of her own letters to Paul, Karla is undoubtedly a masochist and a nymphomaniac. (i.e., programmed to derive pleasure from her own pain, and totally absorbed in the pleasures of sex). By his actions, Paul is a proven sadist and sex maniac. They compliment each other in a deadly interaction that, in concert, amounts to madness. How each of them got that way would be the real story. It would be interesting to know more about their respective backgrounds. Were either of them abused as children? Did they witness abuse, and get a high out of it? Could it have been a combination of interacting experiences that distorted their reasoning that merely required reinforcement to produce madness? More speculation, but certainly based on very strong evidence.

There is, behind all repetitive violent behavioral patterns, such as serial killings, rape and child abuse, a programming that follows a fairly predictable sequence. Genes have very little to do with behavior, other than housing a predisposition for violence that is common to all humanity. An unhappy home life where a child is subjected to constant bickering, ridicule, or sexual abuse, causes feelings of rejection, especially in an only child, or a first older child alone through the first impressionable years and deprived of a sympathetic ear. Loneliness and isolation under such conditions can only result in silent fantasies of physical power and violent revenge. Imagining someone dead stimulates unhealthy necrophilic fantasies, a preoccupation with dead and rotting tissue. The trigger point that leads to repetitive aberrational behavior occurs when fantasy is acted upon for the first time, usually under the influence of some uninhibitor such as alcohol, to create a feeling of fulfillment.

Under either a capitalistic or a socialistic health care system, health - or the absence of health - is a daily obsession, permeating every facet of our lives. If we are to take the World

Health Organization's definition of health literally, (i.e., "A state of complete mental, and social well-being and not merely the absence of disease or infirmity.") then we must consider the whole person and his circumstances. That is to say every deviant from the desirable norm: His inhibitions, his inner emotional turmoils inflicted by trauma, irrational argument, and poverty. We must consider the drug addicts, the alcoholics, the homosexuals, the manic-depressives, the schizophrenics, the schizoids, and then all the other "unacknowledged" victims that we currently incarcerate and classify as criminals, such as the perverts, the pedophiles, rapists, arsonists, murderers, thieves, and everyone else who indulges in destructive social aberrational behavior, and who collectively make up more than a third of our population.

The Snyder-Pert experiment of 1973 demonstrated the theory of the brain's chemical receptor/transmitter interaction, and subsequent experiments have proven the often criminal behavioral effects of its malfunction. There are more mentally unstable people walking the streets than are in mental institutions, and there are more criminals outside on the streets than inside prisons. It is an established fact that most criminals have either an extra chromosome, a mechanical fault in their receptor/transmitter system, a chemical imbalance, suffered dire circumstances in their up-bringing, or a combination of any or all. Indeed, if insanity can be induced by a chemical imbalance caused by the bodily production of chemicals during conflicting or traumatic programming, it can also be produced by an incompatible food intake. (all food being chemicals) The perfect diet has yet to be found, much less customized to individual requirements. When considered together with the proliferation and easy consumption of medical drugs, vitamins, and other illicit drugs, we can assume that none of us can claim uninterrupted sanity, and everyone has intermittent reasons for being classified under the World Health Organization (WHO) definition as being sick. Therefore, on occasion, we can plead temporary insanity for the entire human race. Everyone is a sometime victim of chemical imbalance, and no one is to blame for the aberrational behavior that ensues during that time!

Conventional wisdom dictates that bodily health depends upon a sensible diet, an optimum level of exercise, ample sleep, and a conducive environment, but this last requirement covers a complex variety of circumstances that are often outside the purview or control of the individual. Indeed, all four may be either beyond the means, or outside of the behavioral patterns of the programmed individual.

The planting of viruses in the young human mind is as much a form of mutilation as was the binding of feet of Japanese infant girls, but the programers are themselves programmed by others who have been programmed, and the process is far more insidious and the repercussions far more deadly. For viruses in the mind are the principal reasons we have wars, murders, family break-ups, and physical break-downs, which in turn create addicts, criminals, and general misery throughout the world. Religious programming is the worst distorter and inhibitor of human compassion. Sigmund Freud once said that when a man is freed from religion, he has a better chance to live a normal and wholesome life, ergo - complete physical well being. But to quote Napoleon Bonaparte: "Religion is excellent stuff for keeping the common people quiet."

"Things" with precedence over "self"

Our distorted value system is reflected in our educational system whereby we educate our young in the science of "things" and totally ignore the science of "inner-self." We learn all about electronic computers, but nothing about our own biological computers. We program our children with ghost stories, and realistic, sick films like the "Exorcist." We invade their minds with shadows and fantasies until they lay awake "sensing" the presence of an unknown in every dark corner. And we fail to teach our children the difference between opinion and knowledge. Quite the contrary, we imbue them with bias and fear. We fail to teach them to look inward, and understand their own emotions; why they react negatively - even violently - to ideas that conflict with earlier implanted ideas, or why they love, and the cause and nature of hatred. There would be far less confusion in the world if we analyzed our thinking about ourselves and our emotions.

For anger and hurt are not uncontrollable influences that happen to us, they happen within us as a result of our programming.

Who is to blame for the hatred and murders that encircle the abortion clinics? Can we blame those who have abortions for their own personal reasons, on the grounds that they are being provocative? Can we blame the physician who would rather not bring an unwanted child into the world? What inspired the holocaust? Can we blame the ubiquitous presence of the comparatively wealthy Jew, or their different and therefore provocative form of religious worship, or has alien behavior become a personal affront to those who adhere to their Catholic programming and won't countenance deviation in others? These would-be vigilantes see themselves as a force for good against an evil force, and the Catholic hate virus blinds its victims to the atrocities they commit in pursuit of righteousness.

The root cause of most wars, murder and mayhem is the programming of the hate virus against those who fail to abide by the programmed righteousness of a religion. Within our own borders, we may ask Joe Scheidler, the anti-abortionist and author of the manual entitled, "99 Ways to stop abortion," to name his religious affiliation. Ask the soldiers of the "Army of God" what is their religious affiliation. They advocate bombing, murder and maiming, and they usurp the mandate and integrity of those Catholics serving on the police force by making them allies to their cause through coercing them to place their Catholicism before their law-keeping mandate. These unhappy "law-keepers" are traitors to their own mandate, but they are in an impossible conflict of interest, believing they have no alternative but to obey a higher authority. However, there is always a fringe element of other "camp followers" with various religions, who have been infected by the same programming.

Our beautiful planet, Earth, supplies us with a rich bounty. As long as it can sustain life, it could be the paradise for which we all yearn; we mistakenly blame the place we live for the human miseries and pain we experience from the warped awareness of living with harmful programming. We are too near ourselves to see that our misery emanates from the programming within us.

With programming we perpetuate old miseries and create new ones, acting like irresponsible, unthinking automatons. We repeatedly re-program our future on the hatreds and violence of the past. There is no forgiveness, or "fresh start," not even for our new born children. In perpetuating the beliefs and hatreds of our ancestral mind-set, we can in no way experience the peace, love and tranquility that would make our future secure, content, and productive.

The Declaration of Independence inspired the mass "conscious pursuit of happiness," and ever since we have been pursuing this elusive condition in the wrong places. We look for love, health, wealth, material possessions and a sense of well being, convinced that these desirable attributes are the fundamental keys to happiness. We pursue each independently, and achieve short-term satisfactions, but not happiness.

We pursue health in our diet, and a jog around the park. Wealth must be earned, and so the work ethic was born. We believe material possessions will automatically follow. For love, we rely on the fortuitous meeting, and the magic of body chemistry, and fail to realize that love is programmed on mutual need, just as hate is programmed on rejection and irreconcilable differences. As a child grows and becomes independent, we regrettably feel the thinning of love even though we blind ourselves to that which we cannot accept.

We can blame our collective ignorance and confusion for our aberrational behavior. Few realize that, for all our technological progress, we're presently too handicapped to reach for happiness. We should concentrate on a healthy body from a healthy mind, rather than a healthy mind from a healthy body. We're in a myopic rut that keeps us from seeing the big picture. We experience the unhappiness that is inherent in our lives, but are impotent to correct something that has become an integral part of our inherited environment, for we are not even aware that we perpetuate a lifestyle of confrontation with internal and external conflict. Every country in the world suffers from some sort of internal strife born of its own evolutionary programming.

Speech is wonderfully complex, but it is used in an imprecise way, and often inadvertently conveys the wrong messages. An analysis of mistakes in a large automobile manufacturing company proved the major cause to be sloppy communication. Superintendents invariably gave ambiguous orders, and the workers often failed to listen. Example is stronger than the spoken word, though not always in harmony. It's "monkey see, monkey do, but do as I say, not as I do." In ordinary conversation we speak with the bias of hypocrisy to protect our image. A play for righteousness is the worst inhibitor of truth, for it blinds those who seek it. We are more concerned with impressing our listeners than with conveying the message of truth. Truth is impersonal, often boring and uncontentious. It must be embroidered to be original and interesting. We program our children with hypocrisy, ambiguity, and unsubstantiated opinion.

We speak in a derogatory way of a person having a "closed mind" without giving thought that a closed mind is one already programmed with ideas that repudiate dispute; ideas that are closely meshed in an association of seemingly supportive argument. Ideas that fill the mind can be like a jig-saw puzzle with likely looking pieces forced into the wrong spaces, or a cross word puzzle with likely but wrong answers that present a most convincing structure of contagious ideas, until an obvious truth tears them all down.

We attribute the heart - which is symbolized like the leaf of a redbud tree - with thought and feeling, merely because it is affected by the emotional trauma that is the reaction to our programming. We teach our young that hate is something that emanates from the villainous, instead of warning them that unless we are on guard, it can find its way into the minds of the most innocent and forgiving. We teach them that love springs from the heart, and is a romantic, once-in-a-lifetime occurrence that will carry them to the end of their days, but even as an ideal concept, this is gross misrepresentation. No two human minds are in constant harmony. If children were provided with an earlier understanding of their inner selves, their emotions, they would be better adjusted and happier adults, and less likely to fly off on a tangent with an automatic in a crowded McDonalds.

Marry in haste, repent in leisure.

Among Mazlow's hierarchical level of needs, "the need to love and be loved" can quite easily be achieved with five or ten minutes of reciprocal programming between two adults, with complimentary behavior that is not necessarily sexual intercourse, but programming that meets the emotional needs of the moment, to create harmony and repetitive need; an instantaneous but singular addiction, a mutual love match that may be entirely out of alignment with each other's previous discordant programming. The result can be a roller-coaster marriage of harmony and discord; a ride that sometimes lasts until death do them part - which is sometimes somewhat premature.

But differences on an intellectual level are not usually insurmountable obstacles in a relationship. It is the differences in programmed opinions that create emotional attitudes that are the truly divisive factors in a marriage break-up. And those other seemingly innocuous differences, such as punctuality as opposed to lateness, frugality as opposed to extravagance, seriousness as opposed to frivolity etc, are all inculcated behavioral patterns that cannot be easily talked out on an intellectual level.

Different programming = different world.

Territorial borders are only barbed wire fences dividing killing fields. We must look beyond territorial boundaries for the killing reasons. We must look further than the killing per se, and listen to the music behind the words. For, until pronouncement and challenge, religion does not become a contentious issue. We listen for the discordant sound of different religious programming; early programming that determines the essence of our fundamental beliefs, our creed, our very souls, if you will.

Language, color, and creed, are all dividing differences, but only the last demands either conformity or annihilation. Language and color are superficial differences, easily understood, and overcome in this day and age. Creed is inculcated from birth to become an integral part of us. It is creed that makes the world a killing stage. Different creeds either live in uneasy co-existence - ready to explode - or are already engaged in bloody conflict.

Notwithstanding that diversity of culture adds richness to our lives, and that the church, the chapel, the temple, or the synagogue, (or whatever) offer refuge and harmonious companionship for like thinkers, these institutions are, in truth, centers for the polarization of irreconcilable creeds, differences that have torn the world apart since man first conceived the idea of centralizing his congregation and religion to create an inner power structure.

In a secular world, where such institutions would never have been conceived, we would have spent far less time slaughtering each other. The Jewish holocaust would never have happened, neither would the Spanish Inquisition, nor the Crusades. Ireland would be at peace with England. Israel would be at peace with the Arab world. America, Britain, and the rest of the Christian world would not be hated as infidels by the Muslims. The Serbs and the Croats would not be butchering each other or Muslim women and children, in an "ethnic cleansing" purge in Bosnia-Herzegovina. The nightmare of the more recent Rwanda holocaust, with some five hundred thousand dead at last count, would not have happened. Sadam Hussein would not have started the Gulf war if he had realized the futility of trying to get the Arab world behind him in a holy war. India would still be as one with Pakistan, and not threatened with fragmentation by the Hindus, the Sikhs, the Muslims, the Untouchables, and the other religious splinter groups. And countless other unrecorded conflicts, tribal wars and battles over human sacrifices, idols and witch doctors, would have never happened.

Unless "melting pot countries" - such as America, Canada, Australia, England, and others - realize, and psychologically prepare their subjects for the inherent risk in welcoming diversified religions to their shores, they are heading for a future of internal confrontation and bloodshed. The accompanying bias and intolerance for alternate religions will again rear its ugly head and spawn hate. The balance of power among the different creeds is already changing, and those of a predominant religion will inevitably try to change the smaller factions. No amount of legislated religious tolerance will restrain the religious slaughter that will ensue.

Without the devout confrontation of religions, the homes of intermarriages would very often be more peaceful havens, with less divorce, less bloodshed, homicides and suicides caused by intransigent viewpoints. All four grandparents might be loved equally for what they are, and not for what they are thought to be. The natural alliance between grandparents and their grandchildren would be allowed to flourish in an enjoyable relationship. Mind-poisoning by subtle innuendo would be a less practiced art. Family members would be more like a unit, and more likely to provide psychological succor and mutual support. Children would not be confused, or torn apart by loyalties and biases. In short, the world would be a better place. But such a paradise is the stuff of dreams, and not likely to occur while ninety percent of the world's population are fervent believers in an after life of eternal bliss as a reward for killing the infidel, the non-believer.

The news media of the neutral countries reporting on a foreign war, keeps us up-to-date with the killing score, and who's killing who, but rarely does it go into the psychological reasons behind the killings. They will never tell us that the killings are the result of religions being allowed into the political arena. To do so of course would be tantamount to taking sides and escalating the confrontation, because the warring factions are represented by common globe-spanning religions. A territorial war is not nearly as contentious or likely to spread.

Iran is currently an example of a country permanently controlled by its religion, and its leaders consider that in the name of righteousness, they have the god given right to issue fatwas (hit contracts) even within the borders of a neighboring country of another religion. After eight years and several murders of those connected to the publishing of his book *The Satanic Verses*, Salman Rushdie remains in hiding under British protection. In answer to the free world's economic sanctions, Iran has now promised not to send out their own assassins after Rushdie, but vows that the bounty on his head must remain. And at the time of writing, one third of the American Republican Party belonging to a religious group, is subtly threatening to withdraw their support unless they have their religious say in the governing of the country. Unfortunately politicians are often hypocritical and not very circumspect in the choosing of allies to gain their own ends.

CHAPTER 3

Messages That Shape Our Future

Our life span is so short that the process of evolutionary change is not readily observable. We think of such physiological changes as adaptive changes that happened in the distant past, to leave all life forms on a metaphorical time plateau. But evolution is still ongoing, involving technological progress, ideas, attitudes, inventions, innovations, and everything that sends messages to trigger change in our relationship to our environment. Technological change is presently an accelerating process, outpacing all physiological and sociological adaptation to change, while holding the promise of disastrous potential.

Except for some superficial changes in size - which could be attributable to the meeting and inter-breeding of various tribes - there has been no observable physical change in the evolutionary development of man over the past several thousand years. However, looking over the evidence of the last two hundred years, we can see the very appreciable differences in the lifestyles, that have been the result of changing ideas, value systems, and our perception of the needs for the world in which we live. The next meaningful, mental change - which has already begun in the major universities of the world - will be a universal acceptance of the need for a quality control system within the human mind. As a species, we will start to denigrate individuals who accept too readily those ideas and concepts that are based on sentimentality, weakness and wishful thinking, and as a result we will become stronger, more orientated to the pursuit of truth, and more aware of what we are, how we function, and where we are going. In summary, we will become very different from the present insecure and vacillating creatures that we now are. In time, there will develop a universal purpose for the betterment of humankind that will preclude the incidence of war with all its contributing causes. Wishful thinking? No, just the natural and logical development that will arise from a harmonious unity of purpose in having to start protecting and nursing our habitat in order to survive.

Today we are taking on a more active role in our destiny. Man has become less like a tenant of the world and more like a virus, and because of this, the hospitable environment that once nurtured him from his early beginnings, is becoming a hostile and hazardous place to live.

The quickening pace of environmental change, brought on by our pursuit of knowledge, cheap energy, and a better life, has resulted in a contamination of our air, food and water. Our more intangible inventions and discoveries involving electricity, radio, X ray, microwaves, etc, have damaged the ozone layer, invaded our body systems, and added to the cause of sickness. Our war-mongering propensity has given birth to nuclear and chemical bombs with the potential to reduce our world to a lifeless wasteland. But, with perhaps a few sobering thoughts on what we consider the temporary deterioration of our environment, we regard most of our escapades as scientific breakthroughs that will, in the course of time, bring us an even better lifestyle.

Lifestyles in the last half century have become more sedentary for many individuals, and yet, with transportation, we are more mobile in a geographical sense. Technology and our perception of what's possible, what's right, and what's acceptable, is changing quicker than our physiological ability to adapt. New so-called disposable products are not disposable from an environmental viewpoint. We have become a more homogeneous world society of consumers, more liberal, more unstable, and quicker to react. These are the reasons for wider generation gaps, which are far more pronounced than a century ago.

Seemingly small attacks on the environment are accumulative in damage; there are more devastating wars, more nuclear-testing, more energy-burning waste from worldwide transportation systems, industrial toxic pollution, non-biodegradable throw-aways, unwieldy population growth, and mass population movements for reasons economic and persecutive. The natural water-sheds of the world are being destroyed. Deserts are expanding, and fleeing refugees are evacuating war zones, contaminated and natural disaster areas, in starving droves.

New technologies demand a revised attitude of reverence for the environment, and create revised standards for what we considered aptitudes and qualifications. These in turn create unparalleled unemployment and deprivation that can deteriorate into sickness and an increased dependency on Governments. In total, there are cataclysmic environmental pollutions that require accelerated/evolutionary/tolerance changes, and - if bodily adaptation is too late in forthcoming - such environmental changes could result in the extinction of life as we know it.

We rejoice in a new "information age," and envisage an age of enlightenment - the end of ignorance. One writer stated that the information age will finally dispel the shadows of the dark ages. However, the trouble with the "information age" is that it's an advancing technology springing from minds that are still sociologically retarded. One has only to turn on the news and see the worldwide brutality of the human race to realize that we are badly flawed, and still burdened with the carnal behavior and mythological beliefs of our distant ancestors.

We have each been taught, through our early need to survive, that killing is a viable means to an end. We have each been inculcated, through the slanted lessons of survival, that strength, both physical and military, is not so much a deterrent to aggression as indeed a reason for it. America has recently shown admirable restraint in limiting its superior military strength by balancing its response toward aggressive non-nuclear countries. Anything more would amount to carnage and genocide on an unprecedented scale. The strategy places its military personnel at greater risk, but world politics presently demand that America projects the non-aggressive image of an impartial arbiter.

It is true that the information age has gathered up our available level of knowledge, and brought it to our attention in a categorized and instantaneous form of reference. The electronic marvels of this new age - the computer modem conveying information as quickly as a telephone, the fax machine producing facsimiles across the other side of the world in a matter of seconds, the news media, transmitting through satellites and reaching half the world in a single broadcast, all create a plethora of pervasive and intrusive messages. But each new technology is also capable of carrying misinformation, and - because the authority for censorship could be more restrictive and damaging than carte blanche individual discretion - the information highway is widely exploited with trivia, gossip, religious opinion, lies, manipulative propaganda and exaggerated advertising that in total swamps our need for truthful information. We are being bombarded with garbage, and our very survival depends on protecting our judgement and sanity by separating the wheat from the chaff.

If we are to collectively benefit from this new "information age," we had better realize both its ominous potential and its limitations. The new information technology is confined to the ease and speed of transmitting, storing, and accessing unimaginable volumes of information at the touch of a button, but does nothing to upgrade the content of the message that determines our behavior and future.

Because our imagination transcends our logic, we have consistently proven ourselves to be prolific originators of unmitigated poppycock. Since we learned to wag our tongues and make strange noises, we have been seasoned travelers on flights of fancy, and this new information technology does nothing except exacerbate the situation by speedily bringing the uninformed to new heights of ignorance, and placing them at risk from blanket propaganda traveling the Information Highway, to polarize public opinion at galactic speed.

In fact the new information age has already become an age of confusing messages, of increased government manipulation and control that foretell the termination of individual privacy. Such technology, with a potential to invade an individual's life, is a natural multiplier of the past horrific consequence of manipulation of the many by the few.

It is indeed the message we get that determines our future, and wrong and harmful messages presently proliferate our society. The courts are presently inadvertently giving criminals the wrong message of leniency. Many corrupt police departments around the world are programming each other with reciprocal examples of corruption and self-gain. Romanticized violence and cruelty on television are desensitizing both adults and children with wrong messages.

If we were alerted that an alien world was in the process of intercepting our short wave radio messages, we would be most circumspect in what we say over the air. But in an age when satellite broadcast reaches every corner of the world, when western societies are hosts to representatives of every culture, both friendly and hostile, we remain indifferent to the provocative music behind our thoughtless radio and TV pronouncements that surely insult and challenge other cultures and religions.

On open airways, we convey irresponsible and ill-conceived ideas from a biased and tunnel visioned perspective, to incite world confrontation and violence; egomaniacal ideas of power by non-diplomatic politicians. Ideas of righteousness springing from age-old religious dogmas are sent to challenge ignorance with ignorance. The messages need not be spoken. We send subliminal messages through the television, messages of inappropriate tolerance sent by a more lenient judiciary, permissive messages emanating from government immigration and welfare departments, and messages of example from dishonest politicians that trivialize corruption. Society has adopted a new and inappropriate "gentle" perspective over the last forty years, sending messages of misguided compassion to replace the former disciplinary actions that were the previous guidelines for acceptable social behavior. Permissiveness is more than a predictable backlash after the carnage of the second world war. It is a trend toward a dichotomous and more gentle dual-sex society. (see chap 9)

However, the following provocative examples cannot be attributed to feminine persuasion so much as to universal programming that has swamped our present generation of politicians, judiciary, clergy, and the decision makers within the media; programming that is couched in an ambiguity that lends itself to damaging misinterpretation. With a little thought one can see that the following perhaps well-intentioned messages are easily misconstrued as challenges, encouragement to take devious advantage of ambiguous or incomplete statements that are especially misleading to those without the gift of an acute faculty for reason. They would appear to be addressed to specific and impressionable groups. e.g.:-

1. For the entire world...America will help those countries who are less organized, by supervising their elections, and overseeing the peace process. Interpretation. As the only truly good, democratic, and most militarily powerful country in the world, America should be the judge and arbiter of human rights. It should adopt the role of peacekeeper, and have world-wide approval, with license to interfere in the internal affairs of the less developed and militarily weaker nations. If they haven't the sense to maintain peace in their own land, America must impose peace upon them with its superior diplomacy, backed by its superior military force.

2. For the non-Christian countries... Our missionaries will help you find the way by introducing you to the only real God. Interpretation. Our Christian God is the only true God. He is all powerful, and a jealous God. Forget any other religion.

3. For the poorer countries in strife... America is a sanctuary and a second chance for peace, non-oppression, and comfortable living. Interpretation. Any persecuted person, in any part of the world, can seek asylum in the prosperous USA, where he'll receive Christian compassion in the form of moral and financial support.

4. For the criminally minded... Being a convicted felon is not the end of the line. A fresh start makes for a new life. Interpretation. Notoriety is a type of fame. If you're truly bad, your only punishment is prison, where you can write a book and make a couple of million dollars.

5. For the youth of the country... We will protect the innocence of youth with leniency and understanding. Interpretation. Do it! The young offenders' act will protect you.

6. For the newly arrived immigrant... We will welcome you to our land and accommodate your differences. Interpretation. Human rights and freedom of speech means you can say and do what you think is right, and the mores and customs of your

mother country will be super-imposed over that of your host country.

7. For the poor but militant... We will bring in legislation to alleviate the poor of the land. Interpretation. If enough of us agitate, a charity becomes a right.

8. For the lazy... We will provide unemployment insurance, and welfare for the unemployable. Interpretation. Taxation is so heavy, and welfare so available, it doesn't pay to work.

9. For the violent... Prostitutes are particularly vulnerable to violence. Interpretation. Rape victims, especially prostitutes or girls of low repute, are as much to blame as the rapist.

10. For the unqualified... New technology demands revised qualifications to gain employment. Interpretation. Being unemployed means being without worth, and without a future.

11. For those needing an excuse to turn to crime... Application and perseverance are required to fit into the political and economic system. Interpretation. The only way to beat the system is by turning to crime.

12. For the gullible... The spiritual teaching of the church is necessary for the soul to enter heaven. Interpretation. We don't really understand spirituality, or even heaven for that matter, but we've got to have one to get the other.

13. For the impressionable... One must prepare himself/herself in this life for the eternal life that comes after. Interpretation. Life itself is only a trial run for that which comes after.

14. For the unscrupulous... The aged have less needs than the young. Interpretation. The old and vulnerable must surrender their wealth to the young in the survival of the fittest.

15. For terrorists... Catastrophe gets large headlines. Interpretation. The greater the reported death toll, the better the media coverage.

The news media throbs with such hidden messages that rake the emotions and evoke devastating reactions. Today, there is no respite from the programming. We no longer have to search for answers to many of life's little questions. Solutions and advice - pertinent and impertinent - literally invade our homes. And every speaker, sponsor, or sermonizer injects self-programmed conviction of truth into messages that have no purpose other than to control.

We perceive ourselves as the beneficiaries of a new technology, and as receivers with widening horizons. This is true, as far as it goes. However, because "no man is an island," we are not just receivers. We are also senders. And although groups have developed in different parts of the world, they come from a common evolutionary fountainhead, many evolving through the same school of experience, with messages frequently fraught with collaborative, biased and opinionated dogma.

To Deify Gods

In different times and places our forebears worshiped idols, and, providing they were not personally acquainted with the carver, were quite content to believe that the wooden "God" that stood in the forest clearing had always been there. We have in turn worshiped and given piety to a variety of objects: the sun, moon, and planets, mountains, volcanoes, wailing walls, cows, monkeys, and even dogs. In England, cats were once deemed to be on the side of the devil and the personification of evil.

Failing to find a tangible presence that would give real credibility and inspire continued piety, man resorted to worshiping an intangible concept of a supreme being living somewhere beyond his own mundane existence. Disbelievers had no way of denying his ethereal presence, but, without shape or substance, the religious establishment also found the holy concept difficult to deify - until Jesus Christ became the "Son of God." Christ, the man, in all his teachings, never once claimed or even hinted that He was the son of God. He was in fact a cult leader, following in the footsteps of an earlier predecessor known as the "Righteous one," as born out by the writings of the Deep Sea Scrolls.

There is historical evidence that the elders of Rome, in their scheming pursuit of vicarious power, connived to actively promote the myth of Christianity. Many years after Christ's death, they decreed that Christ should be recognized as the son of God, the reason being that a son must in some ways resemble the father, and so "God" now took on human form to capture the imagination and the empathy of the masses. They also decided that December the twenty-fifth - the time of the Roman summer solstice, the shortest day of the year when the sun commences its return journey to drive away the powers of darkness - should be celebrated as the time of the birth of Christ. The actual sighting of the star of Bethlehem occurred some years before, and has been attributed to the phenomenon of two planets aligning to make an abnormally bright object in the sky. There is no historical determination of the date of Christ's birth, though there are a number of beliefs. Who is to say that the crucifixion and the subsequent resurrection (supported by the disappearance of the body) were not also part of the plot? In those days, the idea of a virgin birth was a common ploy to give credence to the sanctity of "gods." Springing from the sperm of a man's testis was not considered the best way for gods to materialize.

It took another thousand years after the death of Christ, for an artist to finally come up with the face of a suitable ethereal martyr that was supposedly the son of God being crucified. Now everyone recognized "God!" In the last blink of evolutionary time we bought a bill of goods for an indisputable "God," and people are now continuing to feel guilty that he suffered on their behalf.

As unacceptable as it may seem to those of a religious persuasion, the religions of today are mere legacies of programmed attempts by earlier generations to explain the natural phenomena of the world around them. However, as George Santayana wrote, "My atheism, like that of Spinoza, is true piety toward the universe and denies only gods fashioned by men in their own image to be servants of their human interests."

We need to achieve a sociological maturity by adopting a two-pronged approach in learning how to properly define, assess, and interpret information, and also by controlling the temptation to blindly pass on information without assessing the quality and accuracy of messages, whether they be formal or informal, across the room, or across the world. Only when we employ a quality control system within the mind, will we become involved in the difference between truth and opinion. Those who fail to analyze and police their own programming are destined to remain creatures of chance, puppets on the strings of hearsay messages.

Society provides the "idea-environment" for the individual and for government, and this - plus a technologically enhanced news media - makes society more vulnerable to horrendous mass-manipulation from a single idea, whether it be promoted by the ignorant, the unconscionable, or the programmed. We must learn how to control our reaction to information, even to the point of becoming vocal, organized, and political, in order to diffuse its effect on others. We must prevent information being used to manipulate and control us.

Already we are becoming inured to having our persons rendered down to social security numbers that individualize society and provide easy reference and access to government computer filing systems; comprehensive systems that detail our private lives as impersonal statistics. Fifty years ago we would have been incensed at such an audacious invasion of privacy. Today, new generations have been programmed to accept it as a necessary government control mechanism.

Behavioral changes, and changes in attitudes between one generation and the next - whether for good or bad - must begin with the young. But what triggers societal change? What is it that makes a new generation rebel en mass, and go off on a tangent? What makes a new generation different? It is not, as some would suppose, that the younger generation is gifted with a collective insight not granted their forebears. Most average humans are in accord with what is judged to be acceptable social behavior, but each human is unique in his DNA structure, and in his subsequent immersion in chance environment, programming, brainwashing, and education.

We inherit our DNA, and have no choice of the localized environment, religion, or financial circumstance into which we are born, but we are all eventually effected by global changes in the environment. New generations have had first-hand experience of how it affects them personally, and now demand their say in the caretaking of that environment.

The child of today is programmed in the home, and supposedly educated in the school. Brainwashing, or re-programming replaces preconceived ideas with the preconceived opinions or ideas of persons with stronger argument and conviction - whether they are right or wrong. Programming can be the inculcation of either truth or untruth as truth. But programming is not necessarily education. Programming can be the parents steering the children toward the beliefs, concepts and standards passed down from their parents - perhaps ideas that have been passed down through generations of parents - together with their biases and superstitious beliefs that are extremely inhibiting. It is, for instance, as ridiculous for a Sikh to be unable to remove his turban, as it is for a Christian to demand that he should.

True education should never teach opinion as truth. Opinion is at best a degree of probable truth. Of course, many unsubstantiated opinions travel under the name of science and falsely imply truth. Geography is a temporary or changeable truth. History is a biased mixture of truth and untruth according to the recorder, while mathematics and the substantiated sciences are pure permanent truths, though sometimes expounded by opinionated scientists.

In order to benefit from the new information age, we need to comprehend the difference between truth and opinion. Unsubstantiated opinion passed on as truth, whether through ignorance or as an intentional controlling device, is as harmful as government hate propaganda used to manipulate its people into acceptance. Truth itself is not, and cannot be, manipulative.

We project the development of the adult through the development of the child. We probe and try to understand the psychology behind our misanthropic behavior and our degree of self-interest along the spectrum of selfish egoism, from the seemingly normal to the damaging peak of opportunity. We assess behavior, and wonder at the easy breakdown of world peace. Terrorism has more to do with religion than a grievance, or sense of deprivation. Hate messages can evoke emotions, confusions, and insane beliefs that outlive the sense of the spoken word, making more to the violence of rape than hate or lust.

There is more to the distortion of human behavior and the abandonment of conscience than most of us can imagine.

The Snyder-Pert experiment of 1973 provided a breakthrough to a new science of molecular psychology, and more than that, it provided clues to what we are, how we function, disfunction, or self-destruct. The subsequent report by two-time Pulitzer prize winner, Jon Franklin, in his revealing book, *Molecules of the Mind,* received too little of the public acclaim it deserved. However, the reaction of society to such a changing self-perception is ever sluggish and perhaps yet to come, for his book will have long range effects on the way we perceive ourselves, and will have more impact on human behavior than the Charles Darwin report. Whereas that scholarly deduction asked only for acceptance, the Snyder-Pert conclusion demands adherence to a consciously revised vigilance in the programming of human behavior. A universal quality control system.

It has taken the last hundred and fifty years for the world to speculate judgmentally on Darwin's theory of evolution. It has stood the test of time, though many religions still repudiate it outright while others seek to reconcile it with entrenched beliefs. The Snyder-Pert breakthrough is really an adjunct to the now proven Darwinian hypothesis, and must be given equal recognition.

Mazlow's theory of hierarchical needs is less of an affront to our psyche, less controversial and therefore more widely accepted. We are left with a somewhat fuzzy concept of being a chosen species, certainly smarter than praying apes; we're smart enough to have a hierarchical sequence to the satisfying of our needs and goals. What is more confusing, is the fact that, although we may strongly resemble apes, Christianity tells us that we are made in God's image.

Snyder revealed that the occurrence of a thought is accompanied by a simultaneous waft of chemicals across the receptors of the mind. This in itself does not prove that thought is just the squirt of a chemical, (what comes first, the thought or the squirt?) but it supports the theory, long suspected by many, that we are biochemical computers, programmed in the womb, during and after birth; programmed for success, and programmed for failure, programmed for bias, intolerance and hate, and programmed for patience, tolerance and love. We are programmed to accept a particular religious viewpoint, a particular station or lifestyle, and to act out different behavioral patterns that make individuality, productive or otherwise. The variety and complexity of our programming creates diverse and irregular shapes, incompatible with the uniform building blocks needed to build societal systems.

To accept Solomon Snyder's conclusion, however, is to concur that our pre-conceived sense of spirituality has again been challenged, and could indeed be inhibiting our pursuit of truth. Being the only animals capable of self-analysis, we have long considered ourselves to be privileged creatures of spirituality. Our belief in an after-life has been our source of comfort through times of bereavement, material deprivation, and hardship. Even those who intellectually reject the concept, unconsciously embrace it as a possibility. Our idea of "spirituality" has become absorbed by our psyche. Sudden disillusionment - if such a thing was possible - would cause stress and deep feelings of insecurity, not to mention a psychological upheaval that could cause further uninhibited mayhem throughout the world. Like divers coming up from the deep, time would be needed for readjustment. We would also need a psychological substitute for the purpose of living with a new self-perspective.

Dependency on an idea, even one that dominates the propensity of every societal movement, does not necessarily make it truth, and for those who can accept a proposition that negates the concept of our spirituality, a metamorphosis of self-perception is at hand. It is a revelation that will release us from a psychological state of limbo, to continue our brave journey toward ultimate potential and the God of Truth.

Those irrevocably programmed in their beliefs will have already put down this book with feelings of impatience, if not outrage, for the quality of a relationship between writer and reader depends entirely on their past respective programming. This is especially so when discussing religion. If the written word harmonizes with the reader's preconceived ideas, it will be accepted as being appropriate and valid, but if there is no such empathy of the minds, the writer will be quickly rejected. For, after early initial programming, we become deaf and blind to contrary possibilities, and receptive only to ideas that re-enforce. It is for this reason that we need to be particularly sensitive to the divisive issues of the present day.

Readers who are not objective or aware of where we're coming from will inevitably take exception and - with perhaps disgust, anger, or "intellectual rejection" - put down this book without ever realizing that their reaction is the echo of their own long-forgotten opinionated programming. Their earlier experiences and programming have sunk into their sub-conscious memory banks to frustrate re-assessment on the conscious level. There cannot be change in established human behavior unless there is a new and pertinent awareness.

Old age provides no guarantee that we've seen and heard everything. In most cases it probably means that we've experienced the same old humdrum things a thousand times, but old age usually brings a realization that our younger days were spent totally preoccupied in the competition between mortals striving for survival. Old age brings reminiscence, regret, and time to hold a post mortem on life. We spend less time puzzling "how," and more time wondering "why."

To provide conscientious assessment of what might at first seem unacceptable ideas, we must remove the mental blocks from our past programming by "just supposing" that we are unaware victims of misinformation. Just suppose our psyches have been built on man's early yearning for a supportive God. Just suppose we are wasting precious "living time" on a false concept of an afterlife.

For while we have the prerogative to reject, it is also the prerogative to close the door on a new and exciting science that could guide us to the elusive knowledge of what we are and why we behave and react as we do. For in the understanding of ourselves, we realize that we have all been programmed to give precedence to self-serving opinions over altruistic truths, and to place "self before societal systems. While this narrow perspective might have been a necessary survival trait in our early beginnings, at our present stage of evolutionary development it is the cause of conflict, and an impediment to societal goals that were perhaps conceived out of singular ambition for self-recognition, but which could contribute to our individual and collective benefit.

—Unfortunately, the mentally incarcerated progeny of these imaginative but viral ideas, who might be emancipated by this book, are the ones most likely to consider it a personal and hateful attack on their particular beliefs. Human conscience is a byproduct of programming. The decision to have an abortion or not, depends entirely upon past programming and present circumstance, and not on whether one is blessed with some innate sense of righteousness. There is no such thing as innate righteousness, innate goodness, or innate evil. These are just programmed concepts inculcated through being immersed in a complex and often convoluted storm of evolutionary ideas.

CHAPTER 4

Opinion vs Truth

For thousands of years, philosophers and great thinkers have speculated on the difference between opinion and truth. On the face of it, their ideas may seem tedious and somewhat obvious - and therefore something that requires little thought - but that is before we consider the ramifications of confusing the one with the other. To appreciate the somewhat plodding pursuit of a singular idea by these pioneer thinkers of a bygone age, we must understand that such observations were considered original breakthroughs in the general ignorance of their day.

Society has consistently been reluctant to abandon its acceptance of the erroneous and preconceived ideas of the early thinkers, whose somewhat premature and elementary explanations of worldly phenomena remained in vogue for thousands of years, frustrating the truth of the more complicated and realistic explanations of future thinkers.

Socrates, (469 - 399 B.C.) the greatest of all Greek philosophers, concentrated on the difference between opinion and truth (or knowledge). Though he was a man programmed to a religion, Socrates believed and taught that the propensity for "good" was learned through living, and that evil was born of ignorance. Since the doing of evil was judged injurious to the perpetrator, he opined that no wise man would voluntarily choose evil over good, and in the "living and the knowing of thyself," one could identify and accept opinion for what it was. Socrates claimed to be ignorant of everything except knowing the difference between opinion and knowledge.

Unfortunately, the prevailing authorities of the day were of a different opinion than that expressed by Socrates. His teaching, that any man had the capacity for good or evil within himself depending on his path through life, was judged nothing short of heresy. It negated the church's role as the self-appointed champion of the righteous in their fight against the ubiquitous forces of evil. The continued existence of the church required that the forces of good and the malignant forces of evil should be two polarized opposing forces in a never-ending war.

Regardless of the fact that Socrates lived a good life, seeking only truth and goodness, his different viewpoint - which he taught with conviction - was considered subversive to the preconceived ideas of the church, and proof that he worshiped other gods. He was accused of corrupting the young, and made to commit public suicide by drinking hemlock.

In the days of Socrates, an insane person was considered to be possessed of the devil, and all aberrational behavior the manifestation of his evil. When Socrates spoke of opinion as opposed to knowledge, he was zeroing in on one of the fundamental reasons for aberrational behavior, for opinion can be contradicted, can be in conflict with differing opinion, whereas knowledge - which is singular truth - can never be in conflict with itself. When opinion is programmed and acknowledged as mere opinion it is immediately defused, but when it is programmed in the mind as truth, perhaps reinforced by mindless, repetitive ritual, it becomes a time bomb waiting for truth - or more creditable opinion - to come along to contradict and undermine what has become a basic established concept within the mind.

The resulting brainstorm confuses and confounds. But if such a conflict never occurs, we remain perfectly content to live with an instilled opinion, for ignorance is truly bliss until it is exposed for what it is.

It is therefore contrasting opinions, programmed as truths, that confuse and cause aberrational behavior in the biochemical computer we call our mind. Today we realize that evil does not exist as a malignant, monolithic force led by the devil, but as a latent potential within the mind of the individual. Thought does not become evil until translated into action. In other words, Socrates was right.

We have examples of contrasting viewpoints and opinions all around us, between siblings, between political parties, between management and labor, and between different countries and religions. Such differences cause confrontation and conflict. But we can never imagine the trauma and confusion that radically revised concepts cause within a single mind that has been turned upside down by falsely basing its developed structure on an early acceptance of an opinion as truth.

Much to the chagrin of the Jews, Catholics quietly accepted the canon of the New Testament hundreds of years after the Old, with a circumspect transferral of emphasis. There is still an ongoing enmity between the two most aggressive and irreconcilable religions in the Western world. In the absence of definitive knowledge or truth, a cold war accommodates conflicting opinions in an uneasy co-existence of procrastination and disassociation, until once again the pervasive violence of war-hate breaks the barriers of restraint.

In the eighteenth century, a German philosopher named Immanuel Kant demonstrated in his book, "Critique of Pure Reason," that the learning of "truth" is not dependent on life in the process of living, and that one does not have to "live" and experience at first hand in order to gain knowledge. He speculated that though a deeper impression may result from living an experience, our senses are ever open, ever susceptible, ever vulnerable, to the truths, the experiences, and the opinions of others. Indeed, some psychiatrists have conjectured that all such mental stimulation is later reinforced, compounded and enriched by a dream-process of cross-referencing.

Plato, (427 - 347 B.C.) embittered by the unjust execution of his master, Socrates, left Athens to pursue the theme of opinion as opposed to fact. Plato went further in his teaching that the five senses were not always reliable when ascertaining the difference between opinion and knowledge. A round hoop is a circle, until seen from an angle, when it becomes an ellipse, until seen from the side when it becomes a straight line. And further, what is observed as a truth today, may not be a truth tomorrow. Time, position, and circumstance can change truth.

In 339 B.C., Aristotle, then seventeen, became Plato's student, and continued to study under his tutelage for some twenty years, to eventually become his successor as the acknowledged Master Philosopher and scholar of his time. In his avid pursuit of knowledge, Aristotle delved into all fields of academic interest, even touching on psychology, which was not then recognized as a science. His widely acclaimed reputation, already established through being Plato's student, became second to none when given the honor of being chosen by King Philip of Macedonia to tutor his fourteen year old son, Alexander, who later became Alexander the Great.

Aristotle believed that the universe was the result of a great design, comprised of unities of form and matter, that there was a logical pattern to nature, and to all things of heaven and earth. These teachings had great initial impact, and were widely accepted by those who construed them as confirmation of the presence of a higher intelligence. But like all men, Aristotle was not infallible, and was probably the unwitting cause of prolonging ignorance for almost two thousand years.

While expounding his theories, Aristotle went overboard and played with numbers to demonstrate a planned design. The magical number was seven: The Seven Seas, the Seven Sleepers of Ephesus, the Seven Wise Men of Greece, the Seven Wonders of the World, the Seven days in the week, the Seven planets in the galaxy etc etc. And that did it! The Roman Church was so enamored with Aristotle's logic, especially the "Seven" argument

- which it interpreted as proof of a planned creation - that the church elders promptly jumped on the seven band wagons.

Of course there aren't any seven seas, and never were, and the seven wonders of the world are a matter of opinion, which constantly changes throughout time. In fact, the only time he was categorically correct was when he said there were seven days in the week.

However, Aristotle became a pillar of truth that supported church dogma, and, in a reciprocal sense, church dogma embraced Aristotle's teachings, intimidating and inhibiting all contrary thinkers who, in opposing Aristotle, were in effect opposing the dogma of the church.

For more than eighteen hundred years, opposition to Aristotle's teachings was judged as being synonymous with opposition to the church. In the book of Genesis, the world was built in seven days, and on the seventh day "He" rested. And, "Whosoever slayeth Cain, vengeance shall be taken sevenfold." And to Noah - "Of every clean beast thou shall take to thee seven and seven, the male and female... For yet seven days, and I will cause it to rain upon the earth." (Poor Noah! Only seven days to build something large enough to take two of every living species - and with no power tools!) "And the Ark rested on the seventh month, on the seventeenth day of the month... And he stayed yet another seven days: and again sent forth the dove."..Aristotle was the oracle that proved the faith for eighteen hundred years, until Copernicus came along in 1473 A.D. and shattered opinion with truth.

Copernicus (1473 - 1543) theorized, against all Aristotle's teachings, that the world was not stationary, that the moon did not have a luminescence of its own, but reflected the light of the sun. That in fact the earth was not the center of the universe, but merely another planet rotating around the sun. He cited that real heavenly motion must be distinguished from apparent motion as viewed from a moving body, and he put it all in his book, "Concerning the Revolutions of the Celestial spheres."

Upon publication of this book, the church felt the tremors of an impending earthquake beneath the foundation of its pillars, but procrastinated in the banning of the book, fearing such an act would add to its credibility, until 1610, when theory became a proven fact by a peeping Galileo.

Galileo (1564 - 1642 A.D.) had improved on an invention called the telescope. It now magnified to the power of thirty-three to one - not much more powerful than a modern pair of opera glasses - but it was enough to establish the fact that Jupiter had four satellites, and that Aristotle was again wrong with his seven planets in the galaxy.

The church, plagued with debilitating contradiction, brought Galileo before an inquisition of priests, who threatened to burn him as a heretic on the stake if he didn't publicly renounce his findings. Being an unusually intelligent man, Galileo enthusiastically complied, and received the lesser penalty of being confined to his villa in Florence, where it was judged he could do no more damage. However, as all writers know, solitude is conducive to introspection and creative work, and Galileo - though somewhat more circumspect - still continued to write books and make little worrying waves upon the shores of Christianity.

Now, three hundred and fifty odd years later, when anyone who can afford ten dollars is able to confirm Galileo's sightings, the Catholic Church has decided it politically expedient to declare that it had erred in judging Galileo. Of course, if the church can say it "erred," we can also say that in point of fact it committed criminal perjury in denying the evidence of its own eyes and incarcerating an innocent man. It was such despotic protection of enforced beliefs that was responsible for ushering the present "respectable" Sunday worship. Mind control spawned habitual behavior.

When Charles Darwin theorized on the *Origin of the Species*, a chagrined church waited patiently for the idea to go away, but it didn't. Instead, everyone started taking an unhealthy interest in a new fledgling science called anthropology. It grew inexorably over the next hundred years, with the unearthing of skeletal remains of part-human apemen, neolithic skulls, bits and pieces of jaw bones, and other pieces of the puzzle that proved irrefutably that Darwin wasn't just whistling in the wind. But the church once again repudiated the indisputable.

The Old Testament, with its quite absurd tales of magic and miracles, was quietly interpreted as coded wisdom, not to be taken literally! And the comedy of contradiction and cover-up continued in a re-affirmation of opinion over knowledge, and for those who had not been irrevocably programmed to be deaf and blind to contrary teachings, it became increasingly difficult to believe the unbelievable.

It is interesting to note, that only in the last two hundred years has the true scientist lived up to the etymological integrity of his title, and based his findings on observable, recordable facts, tested, checked and verified before disclosure to the world. But this was not the case in the discovery of the Dead Sea Scrolls.

In 1947 an Arab shepherd boy, climbing in the most inhospitable region of the Palestinian Rift Valley that lay to the North West end of the Red Sea, chanced upon a cave that held a cache of ancient manuscripts. These rolled parchments - one as long as twenty-four feet - proved to be the oldest recordings of pre-Christian times. (2nd century B.C.E.)

The search turned up many other parchments, papyri, and copper beating, some reduced by time and seemingly frenzied destruction to a small mountain of jig-saw pieces, rotting and worm-eaten. These tens of thousands of fragments had to be pieced together in order to interpret their message.

The Jordanian authorities, who had jurisdiction over the area, appointed a team of international experts that included Catholic scholars, members of the Protestant clergy, and one or two atheists. The work of interpreting and publishing the Dead Sea Scrolls was allocated on a shared basis, and there developed an immediate rivalry to demonstrate scholarship and to preserve the Christian faith. The struggle soon deteriorated into an attitude of possessive secrecy with each member refusing access to the information contained in his particular allotment - both to other members of the team, and to other outside secular archaeological experts.

The world expected to wait as long as two, three, or even ten years. No one expected a conspiracy of silence that would last as long as forty-four years. It was only in 1991, after persistent international pressure, that the "team of experts" (some of whom had now died and been replaced) allowed photographs to be taken of some of the assembled pieces, and only after the virtual theft of these photographs, that publications started to appear.

Much to the chagrin of the rest of the team, John M, Allegro, author, disbeliever, and maverick member of the original archaeological team, was the only one to abide by his mandate and regularly publish his findings. In his book *The Dead Sea Scrolls and the Christian Myth*, Allegro disclosed evidence that proved that the gospels - touted by the church as historical fact - were in fact pure fiction. The evidence, he said, portrayed Christianity as a second-hand religion, its dogma largely borrowed from the Essenes, and their "Teacher of Righteousness" - a leader of men, but not a magician - who lived more than a hundred years before our recorded birth of the Biblical Christ!

This "Teacher of Righteousness" took his followers out into the desert where they suffered deprivation and disappointment. He too believed he was following in the footsteps of Joshua, (Christ, meaning Savior, or help of the Lord), who had led the Israelites into the promised land. And this Teacher of Righteousness was crucified by Alexander Jannaeus in 88 B.C.E. Allegro goes on to say that gnostic Christianity is a derivative of Canaanite folk religion, Babylonian magic, prophetic Yahwism, and Iranian dualism.

The rest of the archaeological team were appalled at Allegro's indiscretion in publishing his findings, and attributed it to his lack of scholarship and his ambition for limelight. Allegro in turn accused the church of being paranoid in trying to suppress the true interpretation.

In 1955, the late Edmund Wilson, writer in the New York magazine, stepped in and pointed out that the church might be somewhat reluctant to accept conclusions that arose from the newly available information, as it detracted from the perceived originality and thus the uniqueness of the Christian teachings. He further implied that the Christian attitude toward the interpretation might have given rise to bias and the subsequent editing of their own allotment of scrolls. The result of course was an outcry of righteous indignation from the "scholars" on the team. And so it would seem that the garbage of past programming was once again corrupting a unique opportunity to arrive at the true thoughts of the pre-Christian era.

And now we have molecular psychology, a science that proves the chemical mechanism of the mind, and how its susceptibility to possible disfunction can cause aberrational behavior - not evil! The existence of an outside malevolent force of evil is thus disproven by molecular psychology, as is the innate goodness of an opposing righteous force. Molecular psychology has proven man to be a susceptible, ambivalent victim of his own programming, with his future in the lap of chance and not in the hand of God. Until man is selective in accepting only truth, he will have little control over the nature and direction of his own programming, and therefore over his subsequent actions.

Ignorance can be a benign, pre-learning condition, or a malignant accumulation of programmed opinion. To fill the void of ignorance with unsubstantiated opinion, rather than established truths, is to supply temporary satisfying explanations at the expense of logic and the enhancement of the species. The church instructs its congregation to disregard argument and reason - to simply believe and have faith. The doubters are therefore branded as lacking in faith, and the faithful are effectively blinded to a logic that could cause doubt and dissension, for the church knows that in listening to reason, and assessing the degree of truth in opinion, its followers will surely stray to a more convincing argument.

In retrospect, Gorbachev was the most effective leader the Soviet Union ever had, for he did nothing less than lead his country away from a national addiction. Catholicism needs such a leader to issue an edict that tolerance shall replace intolerance, and religious differences shall be treated with love and understanding, rather than hate and fear, even though, like Gorbachev with communism, it might mean the end of Catholicism.

—It is the same religious programming that makes proponents of the "right to live", opponents of the "right to die." This is a philosophical contradiction. Not that anyone can have the "right" to anything, not charity, not compassion, or even love. Only a written contract under law, with the passing of legal consideration, creates a right of expectation for specific performance, but even this "right" is tenuous and frequently breached.

CHAPTER 5

The Programming of Ethics, Morals, and Other Desirable Parameters to Human Behavior

Human Rights?

There are still those ingenuous individuals who believe that civilization has changed basic individuality, that a declaration of human rights makes certain standards of human behavior mandatory. It is their belief that these established, inalienable and enforceable standards dictate one's behavior to another. However, "enforceable" is the operative word, for the concept of "human rights" is merely a man-made political concept, enforceable only in very small pockets of influence. However, in addition to failing to achieve certain standards within our own jurisdiction, we try to impose our somewhat idealistic standards upon countries like China, where human rights are merely the rights of the leaders to ignore the rights of others. President Jiang Zemin and Premier Li Peng are both aspiring to take over from the ailing Deng Xiaoping, who will be 91 next birthday.

American activist, Harry Wu, currently incarcerated in China and awaiting trial for exposing atrocities inflicted on the Chinese people, says that the flagrant abuse of human rights in China is far worse than that experienced by the Jews at the hands of the Nazis.

Human rights do not exist unless they are enforced, and when they are, it is usually at the expense of someone else's rights, and/or self-interest. However, with the advent of the information age, such countries as China are going to be in the spotlight before the entire world. They've been isolated in their tyrannical form of control for too long, ignoring the efforts of those striving to bring some semblance of humane behavior to those who still believe torture a means to an end.

Our expanded responsibility

The ability to create life outside the body - to prolong life, to genetically select and engineer life, and in the process lay emphasis on the desirable traits while eradicating those deemed undesirable - is creating a need for leadership and direction on issues unimagined three decades ago. We can now decide the sex of our child, the color of his eyes, and whether he should be tall, and we can do much more by selecting suitable donors for our petri dish. We now realize that happenings that were in the past shaped by unpredictable fate, now come under the purview of design and intent, and hence become our responsibility. We are seeking new and acceptable codes of behavior to cope with the prerogatives and alternatives of a whole new dimension of possibilities.

When we were creatures with little input into our make-up or destiny, our decisions were confined to those problems affecting self and family preservation. Today, we must make decisions that affect the future and welfare of all humanity, and indeed of every other living creature that shares our environment. But who makes these decisions? At the time of writing, there are many controversial medical cases before the courts, cases that will create precedents. i.e., Who should have priority over the custody of a child born to a surrogate mother who has now changed her mind about relinquishing the child?

Who should have say in the request for euthanasia by a pain-racked patient with no quality to a terminal life?

Who is to say whether judicial decisions will be morally right? And if they are judged not to be so, who else should make the decisions - the state, the church, the involved medical practitioner, or the individual who's body is at risk? Perhaps the responsibility for such public-affecting decisions should be decided by public referendum? But public referendums can be - and often are - manipulated by biased politicians who pose loaded questions. They are often used as manipulative tools by egocentric power brokers.

Who points direction?

We all think of the death penalty from within the context of our own programming. The death sentence of a convicted murderer is cruel and barbaric only if we think it so. This is not an issue to be carried by vote or consensus. Whether we think the death sentence barbaric really has no bearing on the issue. The real issue is whether capital punishment achieves any measurable advantage to society. The method by which it is carried out can indeed be cruel and barbaric, but today, any anesthesiologist can carry out a death sentence with less trauma and pain than a so-called natural death.

There are many questions that need to be answered. Is the death sentence a deterrent? Is a barbaric method of execution more of a deterrent than a humane and painless one. It has proven so in the past. What is a deterrent? Do we need deterrents when we've ample evidence that the criminal is invariably disturbed or sick? Would the proclaimed intention of taking body parts for transplant after an execution be more of a psychological deterrent? This sounds a good idea. Should we do it anyway? China already does it!

Is the death sentence more humane? It's certainly more economical than keeping an incorrigible murderer locked up for life in a small corner enclosed by bars? Is it safer than having the continual worry of a misguided grant of parole, with the consequence of further murders? In addition to the current acceptable moral and ethical standards within a society, such decisions will depend largely on the timing, mood, economic deprivation or affluence at the time of their initiation.

Given the right public mood, the fertile soil of national discontent - perhaps caused by the stress of poor economic conditions - and the unacceptable becomes acceptable. The Third Reich was born under such conditions. Governments change under such conditions. A starving man in the third world might think the sacrifice of a kidney to a rich American a small price to pay for the survival of his family. A poor man might think three or four years in prison in exchange for stealing five hundred thousand dollars a good deal. It's really not bad pay!

There is every chance that within the next twenty years, the non-working aged will accrue as an insupportable burden on the working population, and that such a preponderance of older people will make the lives of the young an unrewarding purgatory. Shouldn't we therefore entertain the idea of euthanasia parlors? After all, there are many terminally ill seniors who would gladly submit to such an end rather than suffer a slow, painful, and undignified death - or perhaps become totally dependent on general escape route, rather than a way for the dying to escape the indignity of either taking drugs through a tunnel of pain, or enduring prolonged suffering.

Sue Rodriguez, a comparatively young woman, was one of many thousands who sought such help. Sue had Lou Gehrig's disease, was an intelligent person, sound of mind, and aware that her disease was incurable, progressive, and terminal. Her life expectancy had been assessed at between ten weeks and fourteen months, depending on the way the disease progressed. In order to avoid the indignities of the latter part of the illness, Sue had requested doctor-assisted suicide at a time of her choosing, when she would be unable to perform the act herself.

Whether this was a case for political legislation, or something to be sanctioned by the courts, a compassionate acquiescence was required immediately. Instead, the courts denied her request, fearful that it would raise a precedent. A precedent! We were afraid that others similarly afflicted with terminal hopelessness, indignity and suffering, would request the same consideration! If the demand is going to be that overwhelming, isn't it a time for legislating change? It's certainly not an issue to be subjected to the arguments and multi-faceted opinions of society. An example of the reaction of two opposing opinions went as follows:

"Stephen Hawkins, the English University Professor, has Lou Gehrig's disease, and he's not contemplating suicide."

"How do you know what he's contemplated? Not that it's pertinent. The only similarity in the two cases is the disease. Stephen Hawkins is a genius who lives in his mind. He's revered around the world and his every need catered to on the university campus. He's almost a disembodied brain, but he still has a quality and purpose to his life that exceeds that of the average person. In fact, a very attractive woman recently left her husband to take care of Mr. Hawkins."

"Suicide is a sin in the eyes of God, and most doctors are against it."

"You mean your God, of course. But isn't it presumptuous to assume that He would be without compassion in this instance? And as for doctors, they have a mandate to preserve life, and it happily coincides with their financial interest in preserving the terminal patient, sometimes for as long as twelve years."

"Apart from the religious aspect, it would create a precedent. Every Tom, Dick, and Harry might want to commit suicide, and any one of them might turn out to be a genius like Hawkins."

These two were not about to resolve their differences. In truth, the geniuses of this world represent less than one hundred thousandth of one percent, and those geriatrics who are about to become geniuses are even less. Such a ridiculous and sanctimonious argument stops us doing what should be done. It is such expressed viewpoints that accumulate to turn public opinion into political issues, and allow the least qualified and more biased to pass judgement on other people's suffering and expressed wishes. It makes us less compassionate than the God some would wish to emulate. It complicates what should be a very simple issue of whether the intent and result is good or harmful. It is very easy to espouse the sanctity of life when one is not suffering the agonies of hell. As a former hospital administrator in what amounted to a hospice, and who believed in and argued the niceties of the sanctity of life, but who is now retired with cancer, I can assure these "experts" that circumstances have a large bearing on perspective. However, at this stage, I have no wish to die, and every intention of living.

The church sustains its argument against suicide by insinuating itself into the eyes of God, and differentiating between ourselves and the animals, whereas in reality only a degree of intelligence, programming, and ability, separates us. Nobody in his right mind would wish to see an animal suffer a slow and tortuous death, but many religious orders view human suffering as the gateway to heaven.

Different ideas, different morals.

Moral and ethical problems can only exist where there are perceived differences between two or more opinions: Opinions of what is right, and what is wrong. What is perceived as good, as opposed to what is perceived as evil. Whether an abandonment of a post is an expedient retreat or a cowardly action. Differences of any kind are in the eye of the beholder, and can be as trivial as left and right, and this and that. We never perceive differing viewpoints as mere differences that need to be examined for motive and the component of truth, as opposed to opinion. Opinions are usually too deeply entrenched in intractable belief to accept close examination.

Honesty and dishonesty in an individual are opposite sides of a weighing scale, weighted with the level of his programming, the level of his need, the level of opportunity, the level of temptation, and the level of risk, and if the scale comes down to prove him an honest man, the levels could quite easily have been weighted differently to prove him otherwise. In the final analysis, circumstances dictate that there is no such thing as an incorruptible man, for integrity itself is a weighted condition of circumstance. While ethics, like meat, can be another man's poison, we are all corruptible - some with lower thresholds to temptation than others - but each has the programmed conscious or unconscious drive for self promotion and gain. Anyone who has traveled the world will have noticed that the leaner the living, the more dishonest the culture. As an East Indian politician once remarked, "Dishonesty is inherent in a culture. Fat cats can afford to be honest." We can only speak of high or low moral integrity in the context of a society's acceptable standards at a given point in time.

The weight of evidence

When the number of proponents of a controversial issue increases to the level that warrants political investment, the moralistic element has served as a catalyst in creating controversy, confrontation, and action. Failure to achieve satisfactory action can only indicate that the opposing moralistic viewpoint has enlisted even greater political support. The democratic process works to sway even moralistic opinion. i.e., The Pope, politicians or potentates, might moralize on the issue of abortion, while some radicals might even kill to promote their cause, but women can still win the issue on the basis of a woman's majority vote for the right to decide.

Man-made Morals

Like society itself, moral and ethical values are in a constant state of flux, and will in time adjust to the greater political influence. There is nothing sacred about morals or ethics; they are concepts peculiar to the background and programmed beliefs of the individual. Ethicists, especially those with religious backgrounds, are inclined to speak of right and wrong as though they were immutable God-made laws. Edmund Burke wrote, that "without supreme rulers (meaning gods) to enforce moral laws, there is no sanction to any contract, virtual or even actual, against the will of the prevalent powers." But gods neither make, nor enforce moral standards. If the ten commandments are moral standards, they were conceived in the human mind, not by a God writing in fire on stone up a mountainside. However, that was a masterful piece of subterfuge, that got some good points across.

Moral standards are inculcated in the programming of the individual's mind, and depending on the intensity of the indoctrination, and circumstances at the time, the individual will utilize his programming at his discretion. Thou shalt not kill! However - with the exception of a comparatively few pacifists - the entire world understands that it's OK if your country is at war, and indeed religious people on both sides of a battle pray to their common God that their cause will prevail.

It is immoral to eat of human flesh! Is a cannibal less virtuous than a vegetarian, or are they both survivors programmed on different criteria? It is on record that survivors of a plane crash resorted to eating their dead in order to stay alive until rescued. Can we point the finger and judge them from the satiety around our dining tables?

It is immoral to steal! If your family is starving, the stealing of a loaf of bread would surely have priority over any moral code, and your greatest concern would be in not getting caught. Circumstances program change in an individual's concept of morality, and adherence to a moral viewpoint sometimes puts its proponent at a distinct disadvantage. The desire to do that which is considered right is just as much a programmed response as your not doing what is considered right, in order to survive.

There will always be different and conflicting answers to world-affecting moral and ethical problems. There will always be different aspects of self-interest, influences and motivations. We are faced with agonizing choices in every facet of human endeavor. There is a dilemma of both individualistic and pluralistic choice, and we recognize that out of pluralistic choice we cannot realistically expect singular decision. Co-operative behavior with the laws and mores of society circumvents anarchy, and this alone is reason enough for individuals to comply with those laws, rather than an opinion of what is morally and ethically correct.

Professional Ethics

Moral and ethical viewpoints differ even within a single profession. A pediatrician can argue very convincingly for the appropriation of government health funds, to the exclusion, detriment and chagrin of the geriatrician. A lawyer has a different slant on the need to establish a conclusive definition of death than a physician. Individual ethics are biased to circumstance. Acceptable social ethics, though transitory and susceptible to long-term change, are the end-products of society's refining process.

No monopoly on moralistic expertise

It would not be unreasonable to assume that the laws of the land are enshrined in acceptable moral and ethical standards. An individual having to conform to such laws, might do so in contravention of his own moral standards that prevent him going to war, joining a union, or even celebrating a religious or national holiday. With objectivity, we recognize the arrogance in assuming an expertise on moral and ethical issues. Neither professionalism, pure intelligence, or even piety, gives one the licence to assume such expertise. Regardless of whether we, as individuals, are reticent or eager to interpret and define such matters, we have in our genes an inexorable drive to survive, to manipulate change, and control the destiny of man. We can forcibly impose behavior, but we are incapable of deciding another's moral outlook.

Inexorable change

Changes in societal beliefs and behavior may be modified or delayed by temporary ethical and moral beliefs, but where change represents a matter of survival, and is an integral part of the progressive nature of evolution, change will prevail over the status quo, for - in the concept of universal time - there is no such thing as "status quo." Paradoxically, though our motivation and driving force is survival, there is no such thing as a survivor per se. We all survive until we succumb. The time expended by different individuals trying to resurrect and reverse society's final verdict on moralistic issues by drumming up public support to change the status quo back to their own programmed beliefs, is one of the great examples of egoistic drive. In the final analysis there is public opinion, - not necessarily truth - pragmatic political action, and social acceptance of legislated change. Only time, and a changing majority opinion that creates political expedience, will again dictate a reversal.

The leadership void

With issues hitherto unimagined, we now look for leadership and direction outside of the church. We scorn the self-promoting politician, despise the schools, and show intolerance for parental guidance. We discard projection of the old beaten moralistic paths, for to seek the way of traditional guidance is to face new and changing issues with limited and outmoded argument.

We have witnessed more change in the last hundred years than our predecessors saw in the last millennium, and the pace is still accelerating. Future shock has arrived and passed, its shock waves running over society in an ongoing reverberation. Past authorities on acceptable moral behavior, such as the church, the family, school or judicial system, are still reeling unsteadily in its wake. Most religious institutions are proving themselves ill-disposed to change, and with the emergence of the need for adaptive leadership, the church is losing its prerogative as the interpreter of right and wrong.

Today there are almost a billion Catholics, certainly the greatest following of any western religion, but their economic welfare and even their lives are entrusted to a decision-making, seemingly uncompromising Papal authority - an authority that ignores the need for pragmatism in a changing and disease-ridden world. Confused, worried, and many pauperized by their prodigious families, the congregational members enter the darkness of the small confessional box, mutter their repentance for their subversive thoughts, and wretchedly adhere to their programming.

The Gulf War is water under the bridge, but, speaking of morals and ethics, Bishop Mahone went on the air in 1991 to protest the sending of more troops by President Bush to the Middle East Gulf. His protest, he righteously declared, was based on "moral and ethical grounds." Whose morals, and whose ethics? The answer might be "the morals of a decent man," but that nebulous answer won't do. A decent man might argue that it would be immoral to stand by and do nothing in the face of naked aggression. A decent man might argue that it would be immoral to send a token or inadequate force to be slaughtered by an unimpressed Hussein. How much is too much? We were not, at that point of protest, at war. We were trying to avoid war. We were talking about a deterrent, and the answer that might have taken these facts into consideration would probably have been, "enough to persuade Hussein that he couldn't win. Enough, in fact, to circumvent a war!" The fact that it didn't avert a war in no way changes the reasoning.

President Bush's actions might have been criticized on the grounds of political expediency - or on the grounds of what constituted a psychological deterrent. And thirdly, he might have been criticized on the basis of a comparative analysis and the decision as to how much it would have taken to get the job done. Criticism could stem from any two or all of the above three criteria. It is probable that the decision to send more troops was based on all three considerations. But to argue the issue on moral and ethical grounds is inappropriate, and mischievous.

We have entered the age of electronics, where communication and information are the main products. It is an era that demands credibility in its leaders, for they are in glass cases, under constant scrutiny. Public criticism of leadership also needs to be appropriate and circumspect, for dissension is also equally exposed, scrutinized and assessed. It is an era in which age-old mores and religious beliefs will have to be revised to be reconciled with the heightened awareness of a less gullible and better educated populace.

New competitors for the "good life"

A new enlightenment is sweeping the globe. New hi-tech communication systems are reaching the far corners of the third world, educating and causing disillusionment with what some had considered the inevitable prevailing condition. There is the beginning of a massive exodus toward the good life of the west, which has the military capability - but apparently not the inclination - to reject immigrants, in an era when isolation is no longer considered a means of maintaining peace and the so-called status quo.

There are differences of opinion as to how to handle the situation, some vigorously against allowing another drain on the taxpayer, some seeing the influx of immigrants as a favorable injection to a lagging economy; some are racial in their objections, others are specific and impartial. Different languages are becoming less of a barrier, and rejection of the unfamiliar foreign mystique is receding before the light of understanding. The realization that we may be educating our potential competitors of the future and showing them the way, is probably lowering our level of tolerance.

The high stakes

The cold war is over, and nations across the world are beginning to see their direction, beginning to jostle for position in a technological war that will in turn be superseded by a more personally intrusive economic war; an all pervasive war that will affect our life-styles, and our nation's respective position in the coming revised hierarchy of nations - the world pecking order - for many years to come. Success will be a self-perpetuating economic level. It has already started with the division of the world into massive free trading blocks. Our very existence, as we know it, will be threatened. Unemployment is a by-product of the technological race, and is in direct proportion to outmoded ideas of what constitutes qualifications, aptitude and production. We are girding our loins for the coming economic struggle, supposedly attempting to reduce our debt load by taxation, to be competitive with economies that can survive on a fraction of our purchased life style.

Leveling a new playing field

Only true selfish capitalism and cheap labor can face the coming challenge. Technology is gradually honing the workforce into an overtaxed elite minority that has the burden of supporting an increasingly non-productive force comprised of redundant, sick, unemployable, and aged.

The reduced work force will understandably carry this burden with some reluctance, knowing that their own potential and lifestyle is being curtailed. As the ratio of productive workers drops, the very technology that contributed to redundancy might prevent our standard of living from plummeting to the intolerable. For the Western world - burdened by high wages, high taxation, an aging and dependent population component, and a mind frame that considers a cushioned lifestyle indispensable - has to either lower its standards to compete with the lean, mean, low taxation, and low wage structure of the newly emerging Eastern Powers, or use a more efficient artificial work force of robotized intelligence. This might seem like pure futuristic speculation, but it is already happening, here, and in Japan, where robots are endowed with humanistic characteristics, and where more than ten thousand robots already exist compared to America's five/seven hundred. In this age of swift change, China will become another technological competitor within less than ten years.

We have the advantage of a developed on-going technology over most eastern countries, but our lead time is insignificant, and we are handicapped by high expectation of lifestyle. Also, western countries that exercise the full spectrum of political choice, suffer political pressures from idealistic social oppositions that sometimes coerce government intervention in issues that are outside of its appropriate or desirable jurisdiction. In pursuing the elusive vote, socialists imply moral turpitude in those with the power to implement such popular-sounding social programs, and again public expectation becomes a costly political pressure for debilitating change.

There will be no room for bipartisan politics or debilitating social programs in the coming economic war, and we should come to terms with this harsh reality, knowing that the elevation, or even the maintaining of our living standards will depend on the winning of the coming economic confrontation. It must be our first and foremost consideration, shelving all other distractions such as intensifying the care of the sick, the elderly and the unemployable, for the winning of this battle will decide our way of life for years to come, since free trade will not ensure equal standards of living for all participants. Only by maintaining an economic superiority on the world markets can we take care of our dependents and our own future. After the economic war, losing nations will hopefully raise their living standards, but for them it will be a long haul.

The handicap of morality

By due process and plurality, it is possible to change the very nature of morality, and give license to a minority to put their hands in the pockets of others. When an individual seeks and secures gratuitous aid, he is - by any sane and impartial judgement - receiving charity. But when ten percent of society - en bloc - demand the same treatment, it becomes politically expedient to regard such assistance as a "right." Pluralism must be protected from the stigma of receiving charity, and so it becomes a "right" for every citizen living with the reality of socialized programs, to receive free medical care. Not that anyone argues the merits of free medical care for the under-privileged, but let us be honest and call it what it is, and also acknowledge that it is a drain on our competitive edge when we'll be needing everything going for us.

Reality

While technological progress cannot be stopped, we are cognizant that governments cannot, on a social service basis, supply the sophisticated level of health care that the new technology makes possible. Under any social care system, it becomes apparent that with the divergence of capability and availability of medical care, there is inevitably evolving a double standard of medicine. Medicine has already become a fork-tongued monster that reflects the inequities of the "haves" and "have nots," a dichotomy that will provide the bare necessities for those without the financial resources to afford the available more sophisticated procedures; a double standard that provides the financially independent with immediate elective surgery, while keeping emergency patients, who have no funds, waiting - sometimes until death obviates the need for an operation. This incongruity would not seem so unfair if those with financial resources were made to use separate, privately funded facilities, and not intrude and take precedence in the already overworked nationally funded facilities.

This inequitable trend is manifesting itself in pilot research projects, encouraged and sponsored by government funds, with the subsequent breakthroughs "set aside" as being too costly for public consumption. A point in fact is the recent discovery that a regular injection of a growth hormone for the aged can bring about biological rejuvenation of up to ten years, but will cost fifteen thousand dollars a year to maintain. Not many couples can afford to set aside thirty thousand dollars a year to continue to play tennis.

Governments, in the socialized Canadian setting, will try to close private laboratories and X ray facilities (usually owned by doctors with a conflict of interest) to avoid further bleeding of the economy. Canadians will see the opening of more government wellness clinics. (hospital-extension facilities strategically placed to take the extra work-load) It will be hoped that the income from such government-owned facilities will offset the expense in a self-sustaining service.

Small privileged groups of elite with either political power, position or wealth, will be the immediate beneficiaries of the new medical technology. Already there are committees formed to decide who will receive certain costly and rationed treatments. The "humanitarian" decisions are already being made, and though the publicized record is positively directed on the lucky recipient, the implication and result is that others are, and will continue to be, denied the life-saving process.

While social conscience dictates that none in our modern and affluent society be denied basic medical care, it would be unrealistic to expect universal access to the sophisticated advances that the latest technology makes available. Neither government nor the medical establishment has the system or resource to satisfy such a demand of high expectation. Ideally, everyone should become permeated with a sense of social responsibility, each sharing the fruits of his labor with his fellow man. In reality, the individual is not such a paragon of virtue, and will not be until need and insecurity is no longer a matter of concern, and not even then if there is the shadow of its re-occurrence. It is not so much that demand for health care has exceeded available supply, but that demand is on revised terms, unacceptable to those supplying the service.

We each have our own conception of what would constitute desirable change. There is no evidence that we all want the same things, that we are unanimous in our direction for change. Politics, the pragmatic following and directing of public opinion, is a fascinating study in itself, for it entails the interaction of different programmed opinions. Politics shapes man, and man conceives politics, in a revolving circle of change.

The ponderous wheels of evolution grind on differences, allowing those with the necessary attributes to advance, while bringing those without versatility, endurance and adaptability, to a dead end. Over the last hundred years, our life styles and pace of living have accelerated, and the environment has become more diversified as a result of an industrial age turning high-tech, and being superimposed on a world reliant on agriculture. Time will see the chemical blending of these two industries, for already scientists are working on what might seem like a science fiction project, but what scientists say is a perfectly viable goal - to grow industrially manufactured products in vacuums. Biochemists are currently bio-engineering technology into an organic mode. Machines are slowly adopting biological systems in a more efficient, less wasteful, and more versatile process of natural selection that is the evolutionary equivalent to breeding molecules for molecular construction. A machine would then become a living thing, and could be made to propagate.

Manfred Eigen, the Nobel prize-winning biochemist, is already declaring artificial evolution "the future of biotechnology." Danny Hillis, computer scientist and inventor, has already "grown" in his laboratory, (through an evolutionary process of natural selection) a number of simple but fool-proof computer-programs. Biotechnology could become such a force in effectively shaping our lives, that it could possibly disillusion the human who is preoccupied with religion. Changes to mankind within the next two hundred years are totally unpredictable.

The marriage between human intelligence and organic technology could either hasten a genetic "branching off" of Homo sapiens in a division of the species, (just as there are different branches and levels of intelligence within the lower primates) or it could play a subtle role in uniting, rather than dividing humanity. Biotechnology could circumvent the beginning of an already evolutionary polarization between two levels of human intelligence. Alternately, artificial intelligence - that would no longer be artificial - could itself become a third independent form of higher intelligence, superseding the perhaps genetically altered human intelligentsia.

—The "misinformation" age didn't start with the advent of the computer. It started ten thousand years ago, when man first started making up stories to assuage his fears of the unknown. Computers have merely made the insidious spread of misinformation more efficient, both in speed and in harmful and explicit targeting.

CHAPTER 6

Early Programming

The way we were

It was a time when plants and living creatures alike had but one pre-ordained purpose in their short lives, and that was the cell symbiotic purpose of nature, to survive and propagate before death overtook them. There were no plans or thoughts beyond the present, for small brain cages housed reptilian brains.

For an unknown number of million years, the changing animal that was to become Homo sapiens stumbled along the dark evolutionary passage of time, first as a wild and timid foraging creature, then as an opportunistic carrion eater, and still later as a thinking hunter at the top of the competitive chain, often hunted, but never-the-less more aggressive and more calculating than the most vicious of the predators.

In a nightmare world of hunting carnivores, survival demanded that man become a social, co-operating animal within the tribe, but the oneness of his mind craved recognition as a valued individual, as a hunter and better provider, as a fearless leader, a trampler of paths, and as a desirable mate for the most desired. And so was born the egoist, the individual with a personal spear to sharpen; one with a need to excel, to gain an edge over companions and competitors, a selfish need that took precedence over that of social co-operation within the tribe.

In a simplistic world of easy explanation, the echo from across the valley was the teasing god of sound, the roll of thunder was the echo of his blows as he made lightening by striking his flint. The proof that the sun-god reigned supreme over all gods, was there for all to see. For the sun-god was the god of light, and sat high and unchallenged, forbidding close scrutiny and relegating lesser gods to stay beneath the surface of the sea, and in the darkness of the earth - toiling to push up the plants for the warmth of his beneficence, or pulling them back from the cold of his absence. The sun-god pacified the rain-god by drying her tears, or scolding her with a warning rainbow. The sea-god, afraid of being sucked dry, appeased the sun-god by changing his color to match the mood of the sun-god. Shadows were as much of a mystery as the coming of night, and were the children of the sinister god of darkness, who hid his shadowy offspring away from the sun-god, behind trees and rocks. Shadows were afraid of the sun-god, and kept solid objects between them throughout the day. When the sun-god slept, the moon-goddess was like a firefly in comparison, playfully aiming her meager light across the surface of the waters to the being on the shore, and racing to hide behind the clouds. The sea-god never changed his colors for her. She didn't demand respect like the changeable wind-god, whose moods fluctuated between singing and howling, and teasing or tearing the trees from their roots.

It was this "supernatural" phenomena of shadows, rainbows, echoes, thunder and lightening, the aurora borealis, and all the unsolved mysteries of nature itself, together with the psychology of fear, that inspired the explanations that conceptualized man's idea of a God and a spiritual world. The idea was undoubtedly a welcome source of comfort and strength, giving a sense of permanence and purpose in a terrifying world where mortals huddled cold and trembling in their caves, imagining demons in the darkness and gods in the galaxy.

Countless generations of man's development were spent in fitful sleep through the dark hours wondering whether they'd survive the light of dawn. Imagination served man well, for it configured the human mind with the chemical of fear, quickening his flight response, providing the figment of a protective god, and conjuring up the promise of a second chance for life in a spiritual world.

Our need for gods comes from this primeval past to permeate our lives with wishful thinking and false promises. It is a part of our evolutionary make-up, and will stay with us to readily accept any god that will satisfy our sense of logic in a subconscious response to fear. The omniscient presence of a god has become the shadow of man's fear.

With the continuum of human thought came the search for man's beginnings, his essence and potential. Whether the related concept of other, better gods was born out of a need for solace and reassurance, or out of a scheming individual's pursuit of vicarious power, we will never know, but it was probably the latter, and these were the messages that man received to determine his future.

The countless little gods, with power personified in every jungle idol, directed the petty affairs of man, deciding the course of his sickness, or the outcome of tribal conflict; they were mischievous gods that had to be appeased by sacrifice.

Such imaginative explanations, born of ignorance, abounded in support of polytheism, (belief in many Gods) but the competition between men and their jealously guarded worship of Gods created amalgamations and eliminations. It was the beginning of the "take over bid" in a monopolistic drive for monotheism. With the beginnings of a scant knowledge of nature and its many wonders, pantheism (belief in an all pervasive God) began to occupy the human mind, but while the agnostic doubted and still does, the atheist - rightly or wrongly - rejected, and by definition, sought alternate explanations.

In ignorance, fear and intimidation, man came to credit all the wonders beyond his understanding to his own personal God of a higher intelligence, and in so doing became a subject of an imagined patron, an invisible, omnipotent God that favored him, and proved it by allowing him to stay alive in the most hostile of worlds. For while survival meant prevailing over beasts with seemingly superior, physical attributes - they were faster, stronger, with long fang and sharp claw - man endured and survived with seemingly only his learned ability to swing a club and throw a spear. However, he seasoned his small armory with a generous helping of bluff, still demonstrated in the lion tamer of today. Man prevailed, never realizing that he was developing a secret weapon that was superior to anything his predators could muster. In ignorance, he continued to give credit to idols, witch doctors, or any intangible and possible presence that his imagination could conjure up as a safeguard against death and disaster.

But besides being endowed with an imagination, time and circumstance were now giving man a brain that was like no other. The foraging on the flat land, and the upright posture that had given him additional speed for the hunt, had also released his hands - those marvelous hands with opposing thumbs and fingers that could grip a club and throw a spear. This, and the need for a rudimentary language to survive, were the developmental attributes needed to interact with, and develop a burgeoning third overlying brain. Because, whereas the reptile still had only its reptilian brain, and the animal his single adjunct, man was developing a third brain, connected to its two fore-runners like computers in series - and furthermore, he had his companions and a communication net-working alliance. With so much going for him, he began to out-think and out-smart the flesh-eaters, until in time their roles became reversed and man became the deadliest hunter and predator of all.

In Laetoli, Tanzania, Mary Leakey discovered the 3.5 million year-old fossilized footprints of upright-walking hominids. They were imprinted in the ashes of a nearby volcano, and this evidence of bipedal footprints divides the early hominids from the apes more than any other factor.

There are certain anthropologists who discount the development of the human hand as a major causal factor for the enlargement of the brain. However, it doesn't take a specialist to see that the release of the hands brought an increased dexterity that enriched both the diet and the lifestyle of the early hominids, providing weapons (clubs, spears, bows and arrows with flint heads, and stone tools) for crushing shellfish, nuts, and perhaps an opponent's head. The weight-bearing hands of the knuckle-walking apes are still heavy and clumsy in comparison to the lighter manipulative fingers of the human hand. Graham Richard's conclusion that bipedalism enslaved the feet does not take into consideration the increased effectiveness in specializing the use of the feet.

Whether the hunter was a fox, a cat, a wolf, a hyena, or even a skilled archer, the result of a hunt was not always an occasion for celebration. It was often the female of the species who saved the day with a meal of nuts, fruits, berries or roots, and an empty belly doesn't question the sex of the provider. Sharing with one's mate is a common survival trait in the animal kingdom, and it was only such co-operation between the sexes that enabled homo sapiens to rise above the animal competitors.

Over millions of years, man came to understand and anticipate the predictable behavior of all the species of animals he hunted. A wolf was a wolf, looking and behaving like a wolf. Every species, except his own, had a distinct and predictable behavioral pattern, but being instinctively aware that he was in some way different, and not knowing why, he remained psychologically insecure and in constant competition with those within the tribe. He snatched food, quarreled and fought, while ever aware that having too many enemies in the tribe could result in his being banished. Being cast out meant either death by isolated starvation, or a weakening that resulted in finally being torn limb from limb in a grisly feast of the predators. And so he tempered his behavior to retain his tenuous position within the hierarchy of the tribe, and in return was allowed to participate in the cooperative hunt. Man has ever been afraid of loneliness and the dark.

When, on occasion, his natural enemies triumphed - when a sabre-toothed tiger acted predictably and dragged off one of their number by the head - the relieved spectators could only conclude that either the unfortunate one's protective God had temporarily been out to lunch, or that the victim had failed to live up to his God's expectation. A wailing plea for help may have been the first prayer ever delivered up to the ether, and a thrown rock fortuitously hitting a tiger's eye may have been construed as prompt forgiveness and salvation.

We are, however, all living proof that most survived to propagate, and gain a measure of security - even to the extent of becoming complacent. For man developed a sequence of ongoing prioritized behavioral patterns that assured the survival of his species. And to combat the increasing boredom of the long night, man became a compulsive story-teller, reciting and re-enacting the events of the hunt.

In the parlance of evolutionary time, when a thousand years is but the tick of a clock, this decade, this century, or surely the next five hundred years, will bring an end to the winter of man's evolutionary development. The metaphysical is receding like shadows before the light of knowledge and reason. A metamorphosis of man's self-perception is at hand, for the knowledge of his past is catching up with his present, and the very id of his being (his inspirations and aspirations) is being recognized as the production of an association of ideas, a permutation of experience that is accumulating and developing into an identity that is individuality and "self." Man's very soul is beginning to unfold as the brain-child of an amazingly intricate organism that is a chemically computerized and self-sustaining biological phenomenon, fed materially and mentally, selectively choosing that which should be retained as the building blocks of "self," and - in most cases - discarding the rest.

Junk-food ideas clutter logic, just as junk food clogs the arteries. Imagination soars on the wings of true and pure concepts, flying like the logic of the Wright brothers, with truth leading to greater jet-powered truths. Creativity, and the attempt to create uniqueness, is more than the inner voice of the individual crying out for recognition: It is the individual's contribution to man's ongoing struggle for immortality, and becomes more intense with his each advancing year.

In looking down the "dark backward and abysm of time" we might comfortably reach the event of the birth of a man called Jesus Christ. But this, in terms of evolutionary time, is but the flick of an eyelid, and this is the point where we start our "civilized" calendar! The beginning of recorded (or misrecorded) history began in Mesopotamia (now Iraq) about five thousand years ago when the city dwellers learned to write. Cro-Magnon Man, between 30,000 and 8000 B.C. was responsible for the famous cave paintings that told us much of their way of life. Perhaps this would make him our earliest recorder. There are scarcely perceptible physical differences between Cro-Magnon Man and Modern Man, and the former had already commenced worship of a selected god.

The prehistoric drawings in dark secluded caves were more than cave decorations; they were attempts to reach beyond the time frame of a limited existence, to carry a message to future generations. The modern-day graffiti artist, the author, the painter, and the poet, all make statements of their uniqueness, and they do it because they are programmed to convey a message for posterity. We are the personal computers that feed into the mainframe of man's accumulated knowledge. He is programmed by the tragic reality of death to give of himself to his young, to pass on all that he has learned in the continuing fight that will one day challenge mortality. Understanding is the synapse, the connection that dispels fear, confusion, doubt, and distrust - the seeds of prejudice - for understanding is the father of compassion and the evolving development that has long separated us from other animals permanently locked in their lowly quest for survival.

Sinning to survive

If there is such a thing as evil, it was embodied in the raw ignorance of the primeval individual, for being a thief by necessity, he was a liar by design. He was an uninhibited fornicator, an adulterer, and when found out, a frequent killer. He was in fact everything and anything that survival and continuance of the species demanded he should be, and because maintaining good relations within the tribe was necessary in order to avoid being cast out to become a singular toothsome morsel, he was also a full-time hypocrite, as cunning as two foxes with a bunch of grapes.

The need for hypocrisy

Hypocrisy is positive, self-promoting propaganda, and primeval man used it to project an image of the good companion, the good story teller, the skillful and generous hunter who would lay down his life for the benefit of the tribe. He learned the advantages of popularity, the beginnings of politics. A credible image, easily manufactured considering the unsuspecting number that actually succumbed when carrying out their masquerade. He concealed his covetous nature beneath a facade of "honor" and, in the case of another man's mate, exercised forbearance in direct proportion to the size and reputation of the intended cuckold. These wary attitudes were conducive to an uneasy co-existence, but it was before the age of reason and negotiation, and mistakes more often resulted in killings. It was this devious schemer, this successful survivor, the primeval egoist, who provided the blueprint for modern man.

Consistent, brutish programming in violence is more often than not reflected in the facial muscles, causing an ugly and thuggish expression. This is more evident when comparing the faces of remote and particularly violent tribes with those of more peace-loving ones. Over generations, these habitual expressions do much to mold the contours of the face. We are all subconsciously aware that our faces betray our naked emotions, and the more sophisticated we become the more we seek to mask our primordial relapses.

Today we don't think of hypocrisy as a way of life - which it is - but only as an isolated response to a particular incident. In reality, we're merely masking our primitive reactions with hypocritical behavior that is the civilized equivalent to poured oil. We've learned to get what we want with sugar, but beneath our mannerisms and affectations we are still the same competitive egoistic individuals.

We'll profess to liking something - someone's attire, a picture, a hair-do, or a book, while our real selfish motive may be to want them to look their worst, avoid conflict, appear polite, save face, enhance our own image, or just remain uninvolved. We'll profess love to satisfy lust, profess a religion because it's the "in thing," or the politically expedient posture that endears us to the majority. We'll pursue a "friendship" that is really nothing but self-interest. We'll exhibit "good sportsmanship," slap a fellow on the back when we feel like pushing him under a train, placate the boss by laughing at his inane jokes, and we'll lie, and say we do none of these things, whitewashing our egos to hide our real purpose from our own conscious level, which is self-gain, enhancement of our own image, and the maintaining of friendly self-rewarding alliances.

Self-examination

This is not about feeling for lumps in the breast, or scrutinizing the mirror for hidden warts and moles. This is about self-psychoanalysis, a look into your inner driving force that is the electro-chemical transducer that converts thought - the electrical impulse that wafts a chemical across the electronic receptors of the brain - into action or verbal response. For, just as an electronic robot is made to perform simple movement functions, so are we triggered by the interaction of different thoughts derived from our programming, racial memories of insecurity, when close alliance meant a greater chance of survival.

Our own behavior, other than memory, is a more revealing indicator of parental programming. Early memories rarely extend to the spoken word, and are usually confined to places and incidents. Memory also blocks out traumatic happenings that profoundly affect later behavior.

Love and hate are closely related. Love represents a close alliance and greater security, and sex is a powerful incentive for a close relationship that might become love, depending on whether the alliance is mutually rewarding over the long haul. Anyone who threatens this alliance becomes an enemy, and where a person stands in the hierarchy of his family has much to do with his subsequent mental attitude toward others.

An only child perceives a threat to parental love when a second child is born, and - unless reassured in a most demonstrative way - will resent his new competitor with a passion. The resulting forced sharing of parental love, or a perceived favorite, exacerbates further the blossoming hatred between siblings. Brothers and sisters are somewhat less competitive with different goals and a sympathetic parent for their respective sex. An over-protective mother might also resent her own second born as an intruder.

Married couples often hate their in-laws for the same reason. Reciprocated love often inspires the hate of a third person. Hence, three's a crowd! If these same adults had never had to share love, they would be less able to handle both marital and parental love. A person might even see such an expansion of allies as a neutralizing of the love he owes his/her spouse. This inadequacy to cope is often exacerbated further by his partner's perceived threat from her in-laws, who may be of different background, religion, different level of education, intelligence, and/or wealth. The hate that takes over is more often than not unconsciously disassociated from reality and voiced in repeated derogatory phrases that have no real basis or cause, other than to brainwash the spouse to a closer alliance.

CHAPTER 7

The way we are

Today, the human race is exactly at the point where logic would predict after being subjected to the programming of its evolutionary journey. It is massively predisposed to believing in various gods of its own imaginative creation. Gods to blame. Gods to thank. Gods to lean on in times of uncertainty and travail. The Gods that once served to give comfort and assurance in a forgotten world of day-to-day survival still survive in our generation to generation programming. We are still in an evolutionary state of déja vu, regurgitating the fantasies of our early beginnings. We are automatons going into the third millennium on our "civilized" calender. And our children are programmed to continue, just as their children and their children's children will be programmed, until the ongoing process of the instillation of reason and truth continues to spread to bring gradual emancipation, like falling rocks before an avalanche of understanding.

We have not yet evolved to our full potential for independence and self-determination. Indeed, such independence of thought is considered blasphemy. Time has in fact nurtured and given strength to this mental dependency on gods, attributing them with all the wonders of creation, the promise of an after life, and all that is beyond our understanding.

We're still clustered in groups striving for strength and companionship, superficially sophisticated and solving our personal problems through co-operative gatherings: governments, police forces, corporations, companies, combines, congregations, confederations, coalitions, and societies. But, behind the need for social co-operation, we're still the same competitive loners, individuals with a need to shine in our own right. We are contradictions, pursuing singular recognition, but capable - as we shall see - of undermining the very institutions we collectively fought to build. Individuality must be expressed, and our images protected from anything that our value system interprets as a detraction. We place personal gain and recognition over team effort, always innovative, scheming, looking for short-cuts that will "beat the pluralized system."

How we became individuals

It is precisely because we have been equipped with unique brains requiring after birth programming, that the human baby is born a complete, but defenseless, dependent blob, the only mammal that has to be held against the teat to be suckled. The lower primates are mobile, spritely, capable of seeking out and grasping clumps of body hair. The more primitive the animal, the more developed their very early functions, and the less need for programming in the living of life. However, as humans with early religious teaching, we start our lessons from life on the premise that this experience is merely a stepping stone to eternal salvation. We inhibit ourselves in a state of selfish psychological limbo, denying our personal strengths, our opportunities and responsibilities to make life more enjoyable, with less suffering, and with more realistic goals.

Parents supply the genes that make the child in accordance with the specifications of their combined DNAs. From follicle to finger nail, the child has all the physical equipment of a complete human being, but, without programming, the extent of his contribution in sustaining his own life is to suck, sleep, urinate and defecate. It is only because he will be individually programmed that he will develop into an entirely original, and unpredictable individual, with perhaps the flaws that go with indiscriminate programming.

We are programmed by generations of accumulative behavior and teachings that were formed by evolutionary necessity and our desire to preserve life in the ongoing process. We are programmed by tradition and by example, by deliberate schooling and by incidental and accidental circumstance. We are programmed by life as we live it, by whim and by chance. By virtue of the permutation of time and chance, we are unique individuals, born of millions of years of individual and singular ancestral programming that has filtered down in language and behavior like a rain of influence in the cracks of humanity. But the most damning and misleading indication of the presence of evil, is the fact that we can be programmed to crave negative as well as positive emotional highs. We can be entertained by cruelty, masochism, and sadism. We can be programmed to enjoy the sight of another's pain, and this is interpreted as a form of insanity, but if programming could cause insanity, we are all susceptible at any given moment.

We are biochemical computers with awesome capacities, and batteries with a potential hundred-year lifetime. We are programmed to live, and programmed to languish into death. But, for the time we live, we are the only creatures with an intelligence capable of solving abstract problems, and - when unencumbered with aberrational programming - self-assessment.

Biochemical computers and their Gods.

If man's biochemical computer, the mind/brain, suffered the same limitations as the electronic computer, then an instructional input that was contradictory, crossed or incompatible with its programmed curriculum, would render it immediately inoperative. Man's infinitely more sophisticated electronic chemical factory is capable of compensating and reconciling incompatible data with extended argument - and madness, like pollution, is only a matter of degree. Awareness of our existence is a product of our level of consciousness produced as energy by electro-chemical reaction, (one would never think that we had this much in common with the single-functioned gasolene engine) but there are documented cases of more than one level of consciousness that divides a single mind to produce the phenomenon of a "multiple personality." Dr Robert Mayer, in his fascinating and scholarly work, *Through Divided Minds*, cites instances where patients perceive life through different windows of consciousness. "They noted that component personalities may be of different ages or sexes than the "host"; may or may not know each other; may or may not like each other; may be of different faiths, ethnic origins, parentage, politics, professions, right or left-handedness or sexual orientation; may have different IQS, brain waves, allergies; may have different languages and dream different dreams; may possess different banks of memories; may have different ambitions and outlooks - may even claim to be spirits, ghosts, angels, devils, or other supernatural beings. These personalities could be demonstrated to be physically, chemically and psychologically different, almost as if they were indeed different people encased in the same body." In other words, different personalities, even within the same body, perceived different gods that influenced and controlled their fragmented "souls."

Today, the countless gods attributed with the ruling of heaven, earth, and the destiny of mankind, have coalesced into eleven competing main world religions - Buddhism, Christianity, Confucianism, Hinduism, Islam, Jainism, Judaism, Shinto, Sikhism, Taoism, and Zoroastrianism. Each religion either worships a different god, has a different way of expressing their worship with a different set of ritualistic behaviors, or is totally occupied in trying to kill each other off. The countless redundant gods of primitive explanation have been relegated to the innocuous and appropriate role of mythological fantasy. It has been easier to discount the idols of material substance, than the intangible gods of our imagination.

The reason we have different languages in the world today is the same reason that we have different religions. It is because of one generation programming a succeeding generation in a particular isolated geographical location. There are four billion people around the globe who believe in a variety of gods - gods created by the survival and growth of eleven different cults, each historically indigenous to different geographical areas. (a supporting evidence that religions are indeed the legacies of successful cults, programmed concepts from earthly sources) Numbers are intimidating. In the USA today, there are some two hundred different major religious bodies - power structures that have split away from other basic beliefs. They program and sway opinion, but never substantiate truth. The more aggressive a religion, the faster the growth factor, and the smaller the loss to competing ideologies. The followers of Catholicism now outnumber those of other religions, including those religions that are far older.

The divergence of technology and sociology

To illustrate how our technological capability has outstripped our sociological development, we have only to look to our technological progress. Our weaponry has gone from a sharpened stick - euphemistically called a spear - to a nuclear, remote-controlled intelligence, with outer-space capability. Our daily range has gone from some ten miles to some ten thousand miles. Our cold inhospitable caves have become furnished, thermostatically controlled, air-conditioned, and even "smart" computerized houses. And the cosmos is fast becoming a playground and sanctuary for those who would reach for it.

When we compare this progress to man's present sociological behavior, which is as primitive in purpose and methodology as that used by his long forgotten forebears, his stunted progress is very apparent, and the reason for this is that man is still heavily burdened with the mental trappings of his evolutionary past. His beliefs are very much the same as his earliest ancestors except for a change of focus. He is very much a fatalist with regard his ultimate destination. His effectiveness is limited by the belief that his future is ordained, and he seeks to enhance himself by using others, through religions, through political appointments, and through hypocrisy. He still makes judgement calls on whether he can get away with theft, whether he is stronger than another in combat, whether he can get in the first strike, and whether he can seduce another's mate - if only for a one night stand.

It is a matter of anthropological and historical fact that Homo sapiens evolved to the beginning of the eighteenth century with the male of the species the provider and outside protector of the family unit, whereas the female had habitually been the homemaker, receiving deeper bonding from her parents in order to perpetuate the homemaking function of carrying and nurturing the child after birth. And so the saying arose, "You have a son "til he gets a wife, but you have a daughter for the rest of your life."

Man's prehistoric role as the fighter for the family, provided easy transference to being the disciplinarian. Of course, for hundreds of years there have been contractual agreements between women to help with household chores, but man always jealously guarded his perceived domain, without relinquishing any part of what, in his opinion, was the dividing line between the male and female function.

These separate and distinct roles have held true in most of the animal kingdom, and the comparatively recent changes in the respective roles of male and female humans were brought about by technological and economic changes that started in the industrial revolution of the mid-seventeen hundreds, and were accompanied by an increasing social awareness of the inequitable and unfavorable bias toward the female of the species.

Many males still exhibit inherited early programming, and are regarded by today's standards as being sociologically Neanderthal in using muscle and size to intimidate the physically weaker sex. And, because of the inadequacy of the male dominated judicial systems, many battered females resort to using sexual placation rather than using the power of the law to ensure a continued roof over their heads.

We still believe that the strategic bluff of a spear, shaken in the face with a shouted threat, can be effectively adapted in a world that is technologically equipped for mass annihilation. Some unilateral leaders, with the necessary power and aggressive temperament, still scorn diplomacy in favor of proving their invincibility, convincing themselves and their followers that killing and pillaging will receive support from their god.

While still metaphorically held against the breast of comforting beliefs, we are commissioned by a lucky process of evolutionary elimination to be the custodians of all earthly life. We are, in an evolutionary sense, sociologically retarded, still quarreling amongst ourselves because we've been conditioned to a confrontation that has long rendered our predator opponents extinct - or virtually so.

We allow and even contribute to massive pollution that contaminates the air and destroys the ozone layer, threatening the precious life we might protect. We undermine our own social systems that might possibly limit the damage, and we produce and sell war-mongering capability that is frequently used against ourselves. We allow unreasonable religious dogma to inhibit our efforts in preventing the spread of the deadliest epidemic known to mankind, while simultaneously killing and maiming to support that same dogma.

We try to smother historical truth even when it's an indisputable happening. We think that by forgetting a shameful past, we can glorify the future. Some American blacks would ban films and books that portray their kind as slaves, thinking it denigrates them as a race. Some women would like to forget the inequality of the sexes that existed from our distant past. Germans would press for suppression of accounts of the holocaust, saying it only serves to keep the wounds open. They are all examples of man's inhumanity to man. We would all like to rewrite history in part, for none of us is without shame - least of all the white Americans who stooped to using slavery. Not that the early Americans were the only ones guilty of slavery. Many other European countries such as Portugal, Spain, and Denmark, all participated in slavery at one time or another, and free-lance British trading ships were among the slave traders of the day.

As shameful as it sounds, circumstances that existed then still exist, and preclude consideration for the welfare of others in favor of self-gain and survival. But, it is only by keeping such memories alive through succeeding generations that we can light their path with our mistakes, and in the process become wiser and more compassionate. There is no changing our self-destructive habits of the future if we forget our past.

Sociologically, we are still children playing with lethal toys, and only in this century has the focus of our attention been widened to include the psychological workings of our own driving system, to realize that the mind is the entity, and the body its physical extension - its servant, provider, porter, and protector. We've been in a state of stasis, applying our inventiveness, our innovativeness, our educational systems, to the understanding and development of the world around us - e.g.: the science of mathematics and engineering - neglecting to look inward with impartial objectivity to the understanding of human motivational behavior.

Programmed FOR LIFE IN LIFE

Kindly Mind Abuse

Parental pre-school programming can inhibit the child and impose life-time limitations, phobias and fears. If you were born and raised in a system that encouraged your over-protective mother to whisk you into the doctor with every little cramp and pain, if every trivial body-ache and irregularity were projected into possible death-threatening situations, then a headache could be a brain tumor, a head cold turn into pneumonia, and the chances are that you're now a victim of repetitive habitual behavior, with a barbed hook in your mind and a psychological dependency on doctors.

In a similar way, society has, by its very industry, accepted the health care syndrome, inculcating many with a crippling dependency on medical care and the need for constant reassurance. Hooks in the mind are viral ideas, those illogical, damaging, debilitating ideas, beliefs and superstitions, that are implanted - usually before reaching the age of reason - when we are vulnerable and in a state of uncertain development, still clutching for the straws of survival. Instead of perceiving our bodies as biological citadels, practically impregnable to the onslaught of infection, we perceive ourselves as targets for every conceivable disease. The art of medicine has been defined as keeping patients preoccupied while nature cures, and even if society en mass were to become suddenly aware of this dependency, it would take generations to purge our hypochondria and be weaned away from the idea that doctors create health, to the less intrusive and natural suggestion of wellness.

A source of health A cause of sickness

A person cannot be physically and mentally healthy unless he thinks himself so, but this is not to say that the thinking of it will necessarily make him healthy. If a man is not what he thinks he is, then it is likely that he is well on the way to becoming what he thinks he is, for it is an established fact that our perception of our self-image dictates our development and actions.

The human mind can be a source of health or a cause of sickness, but we concentrate on the negative, and imbue our mentality with fear. Instead of rejoicing in health, we constantly look over our shoulder for the onslaught of sickness, exercising an ongoing surveillance for symptoms in every trivial ache and pain. Social health care systems that are required to cope with the invasion of viral ideas in the mind, defects in the genes, trauma in the living, disease and pollution in the environment, are destined to eclipse gross national products. But this is the unrealistic expectation and hence the challenge for those who aspire to providing a national social health care service.

Ideas that flock together

Life itself is learned by building an association of ideas - synapses - that are truths. One idea leads to another, and can be likened to the beginnings of forking branches in a growing tree. This book was built upon the use of associated ideas. Erroneous beliefs are branches that will not support further growth. They lead nowhere, stunting mental growth.

Ideas are swift travelers in today's electronic information world, but the reason a society does not respond in unison to a new wisdom is because of another form of natural selection that functions within our species. It is a case of birds of a feather flocking together. Every society is stratified and segregated by levels of economic circumstance, different interests, intelligence levels and educational opportunities, not to mention religious convictions. The situation is exacerbated further by separate and distinct life styles, channeled education, and a wide spectrum of choice in literature and television programming. These differences in choice and participation can have far reaching ramifications as suggested in a later chapter.

If we were all of the same ilk, society would quickly become unified, but our very differences in needs and perspectives, generate productive ideas. Indeed, without differences, there would be a paucity of original thought. If every individual were a replica of the next, identical in circumstance, condition and programming, human society would be like a school of herring, changing direction in unison, without perceptible interaction. Our society would, in effect, cease to function, with no give and take, no offer and acceptance, no driver and passenger, waitress and diner, or doctor and patient, in fact no interaction what-so-ever, because - in the widest sense - society operates and thrives on our differences. That is to say that our differences are the catalysts for interaction.

Differences in our physical attributes, our economic situations, our programming, and our different propensities to accept new programming, are the catalysts for a working society. Paradoxically, a mixed racial marriage with like cultural and religious programming, has more chance of reaching a state of geriatric companionship than a marriage between opposing programmed religious opinions.

Within every family unit that has frequent blow-ups, there is an unconscious bid for mind control by one of the partners. Psychiatrists and family counselors call it "trying to change the behavior of one's partner." Lawyers call it incompatibility, or mental cruelty, but neither the controlled nor the controller is totally aware that what is happening is the result of a perceived basic difference of mind-set, with a compulsive and unconscious need to ensure security by bringing the partner into accord. The attempts to control are subtle and devious, masked by an otherwise liberal tolerance.

The desire to change a spouse's behavior is derived from a deep sense of insecurity and unhappiness that is usually caused by one of five things.

1. A perceived threat of third party intrusion that could cause disruption and family break-up.

2. Perceived extravagance that could cause insecurity when money is tight.

3. Very early and life-lasting religious programming that is at odds with a partner's upbringing.

4. Over-possessiveness in parenthood that shuts out a partner's participation in the programming process.

5. Sexual rejection by either partner.

The first reason can indeed be rectified by constant brain-washing and mind-poisoning against the suspected intruder. The second can only be changed by time and circumstance. But the third and fourth reasons are written in stone, and only temporary compensating common goals can keep such a turbulent marriage going, sustained by constant placation and assurances of love, that in turn serves to inculcate further bewilderment and ensure increased unhappiness. The fifth reason can be either psychological or physical, and needs counseling.

Lives are wasted, and children permanently warped by taking sides in arguments that seem to have no meaning.

Old age resurrects and re-enforces the memory of early religious teachings, when the more youthful "agreement to honor each other's differing viewpoints" becomes in retrospect a "shelving" of basic differences in a temporary truce to allow other desires to reach fruition. With the waning of the sex drive, early programming in religion resurfaces stronger than ever, and the early intractable teachings widen the chasm of irreconcilable differences. Religious differences now become the real bones of contention on a conscious level, causing continued unhappiness at a time that should be reserved for tranquillity and reminiscence.

Contrary programming of idealogies, religions, and disputes over territorial borders have been the basis of cold wars and hot wars throughout the history of man. The exact same "bones of opinionated contention" have been known to resurface time and time again over thousands of years, because programming is carried from one generation to the next.

With the best of intentions

In this complicated and idea-cluttered society, the newly born, incapable of assessing, sifting and rejecting baseless noumena, is bombarded with convention and biased ideas from every conceivable source. None are usually intentionally damaging, and most stem from loving parents, eager to give their offspring the protection of pre-school programming, or the knowledge and guidance necessary for his journey through life's hostile maze. Some parents go further, and try to prepare their children for a perceived spiritual world beyond. Parents who have been made victims of mental incarceration invariably take their children into the same small cage, perceiving their selfish possessiveness that inhibits mental growth from outside influence as being protective love.

Parental guidance is of course essential in the early years, but some parents tend to pursue the role of the eternal oracle and in so doing program their children to continually seek leadership. The world is full of such followers willing to lay down their lives for a leader's cause. Nature makes our newborn a human sponge, avidly absorbing every scrap of information in a blind, primordial struggle to gain a toe-hold on life, and among the avalanche of essential information, parents inculcate their own opinions, confusions, and inner conflicts.

We are born with neither skill, aptitude, nor interest. An interest comes through favorable exposure. An aptitude comes through exposure and participation. A skill comes through exposure, participation, and repetitive perseverance. Some might inherit a propensity or physical advantage toward certain achievements, but without exposure to one of our five senses, we are as blank as a roll of unused film; we are without aptitude, skill, or even aberrational behavior.

Learning the language is almost a perfunctory requisite to the sixteen years of gathering the necessary life-permitting knowledge that leads to adulthood. Words are the basis of ideas and expressed opinions, and it is interesting to note that Professor Robert H. Seashore, a past chairman of the department of psychology at North Western University, demonstrated in his studies some two decades ago, that the average child of six begins to learn an average of 5,000 new words per year, and at ten knows the meaning of 34,300 words. But though the technological advances in medicine, communication, and computerization, have added some two hundred new words to our vocabulary every year, the average adult has still only got a vocabulary of approximately 50,000 words, which - without conscious effort to improve - remains more or less static throughout his life.

Francine Patterson and Eugene Linden, in their fascinating book entitled *The Education of Koko*, wrote of the long period of programming to inculcate a young female gorilla with the human attribute of language. At the time of reading of Koko's progress, she had successfully comprehended some six hundred words in sign, picture and oral language, demonstrated a lively sense of humor using these mediums, and an ability to adapt her newly acquired skills to communicate with another male gorilla.

Anything seen, heard, smelled, touched or tasted, is the programming grist for the five-sensed mill that is common to all living animals, but it is the memory, the association of ideas, the deductions, human relationships, moods, values, behavioral patterns and prejudices, that produce the distinctive interpretations used in our awareness. They are the mixed permutations that distinguish and decide our behavior as human individuals. And the earlier the programming, the more deeply entrenched our beliefs and subsequent behavior.

A child of our distant past probably matured in eight or nine years, and had a life expectancy of around thirty-two or thirty-five years, whereas the normal pampered child born into the sophisticated American society of today takes twice as long to mature, and can expect to live more than twice as long. The wild canine lives around eight or nine years, but given the advantage of domesticity with man, often lives into its late teens. This would seem to support the somewhat obvious conclusion that environment and programming have a profound effect on longevity.

For proof of the deep and irrevocable effects of early programming we have only to refer to the extreme cases of physical damage caused by submersion in alien environments. In November of 1990, Reuter's correspondent in Johannesburg reported the rescue of a blond, blue-eyed child, who had been confined and reared in a kennel with the family dog as his only companion. The child was permanently retarded, and could only bark and whimper in unison with the dog. Though around six years of age, he was unable to walk, and was crippled through keeping his fingers tucked under to simulate paws. The story of Tarzan makes for entertaining reading, but in reality this unfortunate creature would be hopelessly retarded, and permanently imprinted with ape-like behavior.

Many young children who are allowed to habitually watch violence on television have parents who claim that this form of entertainment never caused aberrational behavior in their own lives. However, these parents are discounting the avalanche of counteracting influences that created their own individuality.

Pre-birth programming

We are indeed partially programmed from conception, for within the double helix of the DNA molecule lies the blueprint for the individual to be. Within that blueprint lies the determination of the physiological features, attributes and susceptibilities of bodily functions, personality, response and interaction with the environment within which we are born. We know that all life is composed of chemical molecules, and it is the structure of the chemical and not the source of the chemical that determines its function. Programming for survival and procreation lies within our lower reptilian brain, and is passed in the genes from the mother to the child within the womb. This form of racial memory is consistent with the "before birth programming" of the simpler forms of life.

Other animals are not so dependent on after-birth programming as humans, or as susceptible to the flaws of indiscriminate programming in the later learning process. The presence of the developing fetus in the womb usually programs the carrier to a caring attitude. It is not surprising therefore that biological mothers, acting as surrogates, have difficulty in parting with their new borns - in spite of the initially agreed upon fee for womb-service.

Beware the chance remark

A parent's chance remark, or exposure to a different lifestyle, can each constitute early programming, and can decide whether a child accepts or rejects a lowly position in society's pecking order. A frustrated parent who screams at a child that he'll never amount to anything, may be planting a self-destructive inhibition, a self-fulfilling prophesy, by perpetuating his own negative programming. Such programming can occur in a fleeting moment of indiscretion. It is an insidious and ever-present influence upon our future self-perception, for once a person has been programmed to a low self-esteem - whether by failure, fact or fantasy - he can become the most sensitive, the most difficult, the most confrontational of individuals, compensating for his imagined or real inadequacy with aggression.

An egoist thinks only of himself. An egocentric is hard to tolerate because he thinks the universe rotates around himself. But an egomaniac is a dangerous and inhibited aggressor. (Chapter One) On first appearance, and in the early years, an egomaniac is a person of low self-esteem, guarded, reticent, and not likely to promote a relationship. As a close friend, if such a thing is possible, he is abrasive, without humor, and easily offended. As a family member, he is unable to accept suggestions or constructive criticism without suspecting that it stems from hate rather than from love and concern for his welfare. His early behavior is an unspoken plea to the world that he be treated specially, that we make allowances, and though "different," he is really harmless, lovable - in fact, brilliant. But to accommodate this plea is to reinforce his degradation and despair, for only by recognizing and repairing one's own fences can we be made whole. Recognition of what and why we are, and getting to the root cause of our self-denial, is understanding, and ninety percent of the cure.

It is for reasons of preventing such damage, that irrational and intransigent beliefs must not be implanted in the young to become impediments to the development of logical thinking and reasoning by the later adult. These beliefs are also damaging to a relationship with those who have not had the disadvantage of such early opinionated programming, and who now reject such dogma on the basis of reason. Whether a person's value system is based on programmed truth or opinion, the old adage, "to thine own self be true," is still the prescription for self-respect, and this is why it is practically impossible to separate a person from his early programming.

Though still in the far distance, there will come a time when we acknowledge and nurture the "sensitive early period of development" i.e., the first six years, and be truly selective in early programming in order not to damage the child and the society of which he is an essential part. The science of epistemology - the study of the origins of knowledge - will grow with increasing recognition that most early teaching of what we are, how we function and relate to the world around us, is based on mere opinion, and often no more accurate than mythological folklore.

Hopes and aspirations

We carry an immortal spark in our progeny that is the continuing pursuit of knowledge and truth, for we instinctively know that ultimately we will only be fulfilled at the very pinnacle of universal knowledge. We view evolutionary change as a physical transformation, or biological adaptation, but all change, whether in mental processes, perception or interpretation, has its evolutionary impact. Fundamental adjustments in the perception of what we are, how we function, interact or become motivated, are essential stepping stones to the goal of ultimate truth. But even greater obstacles block mass acceptance of these revised perceptions, for change and progress do not march in uniform agreement across the globe. Changes in the way we perceive ourselves go to the very root of the conglomeration of inter-related systems, rules, and a modicum of conformity we call society.

If we are to believe the two-time Pulitzer prize winner, Jon Franklin, writing on the Snyder-Pert experiment of 1973, in his book, "Molecules of the Mind," each one of us is a biological machine, defective or otherwise, programmed by genetic and environmental influence. A defective gene means a defective enzyme, and in turn a defective molecule and defective chemical reaction, resulting in incoherent, criminal, or twisted thought.

Therefore, will genetic engineering, combined with selective programming, make us model citizens?

In the constant sifting process for the building blocks of truth - of which we are fundamental components - we need to shed that inhibiting part of our psyche that we consider our spirituality. For that psychological crutch has long served its purpose in the early preservation of the species, and must now be relinquished before it turns into a permanent prosthetic to further distort the reflection of "self." For these old self-perceived images, these incompatible differences in belief and purpose of our function, confound the logic of credibility.

In the past, language, race, color and creed, were all differences that failed to immediately compute, but differences in language are becoming less of a barrier to communication, and the individual realizes that the problems of color and race are superficial to mankind as a species, and may in fact enhance his potential in certain cases.

However, the differences in the programming of religious beliefs go to the very core of man's self-perception, and will not be so easily reconciled. Religion is to man what the pacifier is to the young child; if he is allowed to retain it past a certain time in his evolutionary growth, it will result in distortion of independent thought and malformation, but try to take it away from him and one can expect a tantrum.

Man's interest tends to wane beyond the time frame of his own existence, and weaning future generations away from the comfort of religion will take many years on the evolutionary clock. Sociologically, man is presently too preoccupied playing the elimination game of musical chairs with the different religions, as he seeks to justify his own faith by persuading others to relinquish theirs. As one religion swallows, allies with, or eclipses another - such as the Methodists, Presbyterians, Congregational Churches of Canada, General Council of Local Union Churches, and the Evangelical United Brethren Church, all amalgamating as the United Church in order to avoid separate extinction - we move closer to a singleness of belief.

But the ultimate permanent take-over by any one single religion would be tantamount to universal acceptance of a psychological crutch as the norm. Religion is comforting in an uncertain world, as are all regular, repetitive rituals - whether they be smoking, drinking, praying, receiving sacrament from the priest, or getting reassurance from the doctor. We all tend to seek the comfort of the familiar, and it becomes our rut and behavioral pattern for self-programming. On occasion it can also become our chemical dependency, for the brain is also a chemical factory, and habitual pleasure-seeking behavior sends a spray of the required chemical across the receptors of the mind in response to the repetitive pleasure-seeking activity that becomes our addiction and way of life.

It is a known fact that jogging can become as much an addiction as masturbation. Karl Marx said that religion is the opium of the masses, implying that we can become addicted to religion. Like a broken phonograph record, addiction is a repetitive flaw in the flow of life. It is a malfunction and a sickness. But in truth there is little in the habits of life to which we cannot become addicted.

We are chemically made and chemically activated. Adrenalin flows to make us active, melatonin drips to make us sleep. Experiments with animals have shown that because the body-chemistry adapts to its own structural pattern, a female child given male hormones at a very early age will exhibit male behavior throughout the rest of her life. Similarly, if a male child is given serotonin, he will become more aggressive, and, once risen in the pecking order of society, will retain that position with continued bodily production of that chemical, for it is proven that this particular chemical distinguishes the dominant male among the lower primate pack.

Oxford university has been in existence since the year 1117 and, together with Cambridge and Eaton, has been recognized by world leaders as an institution famous for turning out world leaders. Anyone not having the benefit of such a privileged education has less chance of becoming a Minister of the Crown, Prime Minister, or President. America is particularly interested in Oxford for its system of Rhode scholarships for American students. Clinton was a Rhode scholar.

To this day these institutions are successful, and many attribute the success to the specialized knowledge being taught. But there are now many universities around the world that are just as comprehensive in their curriculum, and fail to reach a commensurate success rate. The inherited genes of leadership have been cited as the reason for these English institutions consistently turning out world leaders, but this doesn't follow in other jurisdictions. While the opportunity that is presented by the students" inherited status could of course be another factor, there is more to the story. Although not proven, the phenomenal number of world leaders turned out by these institutions can probably also be attributed to the inculcation from early childhood to a prevenient response to leadership, together with the programming of expectation, that in total results in the bodily production of serotonin. It would be an interesting exercise to check out where many world leaders of today were educated, especially those from the now defunct parts of the old British Empire.

Sexual orientation

In the early stages of pregnancy the fetus is female, developing male genitalia only in the later stages. But even after the biological birth of a male child, sexual orientation is an ambivalent site somewhere along the spectrum between male and female. Sexual desire and orientation originate in the brain, and need the subtle programming of the male as a role model to reinforce maleness. A female role model, or an ambivalent or poor male model, can result in homosexuality in the male child. After approximately ten years of having a weak or perverted role model, it becomes practically impossible to re-orientate a male youth to heterosexual desire. Two gay males, or gay females living together, present a high risk of perverting an adopted child living within that unnatural lifestyle, but this is not to say that consenting adults should not be allowed all the other privileges of normal societal members.

The truth is, most children experience some sort of passing homosexual or lesbian relationship in the course of growing up, but - depending on the strength, and number of occasions of this programming - their sexual orientation is weakened but not usually changed by the adventure. Parents prudently supply separate bedrooms for brother and sister while permissively allowing brothers to share the same bed through puberty - the age of sexual experimentation! Similarly, sisters often share the same bed during puberty, nurturing lesbianism, and once programmed to the pleasures of sexual perversion these unfortunates go forth to spread their affliction, and perhaps damage their own future marriages. If parents suspect such undesirable behavior it would be wise to explain the dangers of such experimentation.

Autopsies carried out on the brains of homosexuals produced what has been considered evidence of fundamental genetic differences, but this might not always be the case, though it is undoubtedly what homosexuals would like to hear. Genetic impairment has been argued on the ground that homosexuality often runs in families, but it runs in families because one person's behavior is another person's programming. Failure to have a male role model, or having a defective role model, results in having a chemical production imbalance. The brain produces the required chemicals to perpetuate a gratifying or addictive behavior, which over time brings about structural re-configurations within the brain that could be later misconstrued as a genetic malformation. While the brain is a magical chemical factory that produces certain behaviors, so does that repetitive behavior re-enforce the production of that chemical. Sexual perversion is thus both addictive and contagious.

Every successful species of animal is endowed with the chemical configurations for repetitive self-sustaining behavioral patterns. It is nature's method of guidance to the preservation and perpetuation of a species. A dog will seek out a bitch on heat, but failing that happy circumstance will try to impose his pleasure-seeking activity on a more submissive and smaller dog, or a cushion, or even his master's leg. And it is very certain that once rewarding satisfaction is derived from such an activity, repetitive behavior will become habitual, even to the exclusion of seeking a bitch in heat. Homosexuality in man is a perversion of the normal drive to procreate, and when preferred to coitus, is, except in the most exceptional cases of birth defect, the result of ingrained early programming.

Today, homosexuals are coming out of the closet in droves. It's apparently a much larger closet than at first suspected, housing a whole production line, but this is only the impression caused by the fact that "coming out" has become an occasion for public announcement. What is not so public is how they got in the closet in the first place. Many, but not all, will remember their first homosexual experiences that started their programming in aberrational behavior. It is probably a sad and regretful experience they would sooner forget.

Apparently homosexuals are not the only ones who have been living in closets. In the polite society of the days of yore, men were considered to be sexually lusting beasts, and women in general were programmed to convey the impression that they endured sex rather than enjoyed it. Today, women discuss on open airways how to titillate the male, and achieve the most enjoyable orgasm. And failing that, how to effectively masturbate. One can hardly settle down to a late hour of flipping the remote control before bedtime without learning of erogenous zones hitherto unsuspected, but which have suddenly become as numerous as the flavors of ice-cream. The path of the sperm has become as familiar as the way to the washroom. One knows it's time to retire when the little doctor-lady who kept saying penis and vagina with such a delightful accent, suddenly starts advising us to buy a "Honda Prelewd."

Homosexual child molestation is as old as prostitution. The only reason we've heard so much about it in the last decade, is because we've suddenly been plunged into the blossoming of an open society, where adults are no longer afraid to disclose their childhood experiences, or to confront their molesters. Disclosures sometimes go as far back as their early childhood, but the chemical byways of perverted brain configurations have been made, and a child continuously sexually molested is doomed to pursue his own perverted search for victims. Child molestation is another addiction that in time chemically alters the configuration of the malleable brain. Man is a sexual, pleasure-loving animal, and pursues gratification whenever desire and opportunity coincide. A frustrated male, so hooked on perversion, will repeatedly pursue such a lifestyle even after exposure has made him a social outcast, for he is a victim of irrevocable programming, and beyond help, no matter how he may agonize for rehabilitation. Indeed, in circumstances of complete isolation, he could just as well be a chimpanzee, goat, or pony molester, but neither one is genetically deformed.

A teenager tells his friend that masturbation makes hair grow on the palm of a hand. When the gullible one anxiously scrutinizes his palm, raucous laughter tells him he's exposed his darkest secret. Chronic masturbation might not make hairs grow on the palm, but it does make its own unique brain configuration. The trouble is we are getting into an area of such prevalence, that it is difficult to distinguish between the norm and the exception.

If man has such a thing as an Achilles heel, it is located in his mind, not at the extremity of his foot. For, while this biochemical computer (the brain/mind) can appreciate the far-reaching complexity of its own function - its versatility, volatility, its manifestation as a personality with moods, emotions, tears, laughter and sorrow - it is also aware of its vulnerability to the trauma of outside stimulus. A personal tragedy, such as the death of a spouse, can release a lethal combination of chemicals that can prompt an internal attack on the vital organs within the body it controls.

Suicide can be either active or passive, conscious or unconscious. It can be the result of an impulse that dictates immediate self-destructive action, or it can be induced by a gradual, unconscious process that causes deterioration and organ disfunction. Thought is only a squirt of a chemical across the receptors in the mind, but conversely, outside stimulus, (i.e., darkness, enclosed space, life-threatening height, etc) when associated with past programming, can dictate the selection and combination of these chemicals, producing fear without cause or substance, an illogical phobia that is our Achilles heel.

But no living thing can survive without being programmed for living, whether it be in the seed or in the life as it is lived. From conception to death we are programmed to inurement against the devastating reality of our own mortality, and only age and the breakdown of vital bodily function can sensitize us on a conscious level to our fleeting existence. But in that awareness, we are psychologically prepared, our immune system triggered to withdraw, to leave us more vulnerable. Like leaves from a tree, we are part of an endless cycle of decay and renewal, programmed to live with compassion or cruelty, to procreate and die.

As temporary entities, programmed individually, we are capable of any unpredictable and inhuman behavior that might be judged despicable and unacceptable by other programmed standards. Know thyself and weep for mankind, for to know thyself is to know that, given the programming and circumstances, you are capable of any atrocity or cruelty, as can be demonstrated by the recorded behavior and programming of certain egomaniacs. From the certainty of a lifetime of relatively benign programming we find this hard to believe, for you and I have been spared the ignominious fate of being out of accord with the mores of society. Our programming is our morality, our predictability, and the measure of our harmonious relationship with society. We are indeed among the fortunate, for the hooks in our mind are not as yet festering.

From the beginning, the human mind has absorbed whatever incidental programming that came along. But just as we are at last becoming diet conscious, i.e.; becoming particular about the food we eat, so in the age of computer development are we beginning to recognize the emerging image of the workings of the human brain, and to be aware of what we feed our minds. We are beginning to regulate and select our own programming. For, unlike computers, we are capable of programming ourselves, providing we have the awareness to question the ideas of others, and can get over our own early programming. Unless we realize what we are, how we are the product of our programming, and how and why we function, we won't know where we're going. Unless we take action to initiate an all-encompassing outlook, and an inward sifting for truth, we will forever remain unaware, and stay sociologically immature.

However, evolutionary change is subject to deviations and braking mechanisms, and societal change is inhibited by more than the chaos of individual egoism and the programming of conflicting opinions as truths. It is also inhibited by our historical and ongoing programming, the mores of mankind, the moral and ethical perceptions that bind societies to fixed behavioral patterns, as discussed in Chapter 5.

CHAPTER 8

Programmed Not to Question

The ghost of past programming

The effects of early, indiscriminate programming upon the unconscious level will persist as an irrevocable echo throughout the life of the subject, regardless of a subsequent capacity to reason and to intellectually reject at the conscious level. Programming becomes hypnotism when the subject is induced to completely surrender himself. All religions preach blind trust. It is the beginning of a bid for complete mind control, and has become an integral part of all religious teaching on the premise that without blind trust, there is no faith. The concept is today conscientiously followed by both congregation and preacher alike, but it was without doubt originally conceived and used by individuals who fully understood its potential for power and control.

The writer was programmed from birth to believe in the existence of a hereafter, and when the computer broke down during the writing of this book, erasing the first chapter, the immediate thought that popped into mind was that God was intervening to prevent such subversive writing. Intellectually we can laugh at our own superstitions and early programming, but the shadow of an omnipotent presence will forever be with us, for unfortunately we have no erase button. Erroneous beliefs, implanted early as truths become irrevocably fused as an integral part of our being, and can only be weakened by tedious and traumatic reprogramming.

We are prone to think of ideas and opinions as transitory intangibles that can be accepted or rejected at will, but when absorbed as truths before the age of reason, they are like definitive fish-hooks, giving us a mental foundation and inhibiting alternate ideas. Any beliefs so laid in a concrete called "truth," color the future of our very existence to the point where dispute, ridicule or disbelief becomes a personal affront, an intolerable blasphemy that incenses as if denying some immutable law. Therefore, after the age of our "initial early programming," we are not free to accept or reject certain ideas on their merit, because our preconceived ideas frustrate impartial assessment.

The dictators that govern with regimes of fear use youth movements to inculcate an early and lifetime loyalty to their political control, even to the extent of turning children against their own families.

Mao Tse-tung, chairman of the Chinese communist party, had his "Young Pioneers," his "Communist Youth Movement," and the "Party," to cover all ages and ensure compliance with his little red book of doctrines. Hitler, Benito Mussolini, and Fidel Castro all had their youth movements for the early programming of their people. And the same principle of early programming applies to religion. In fact, the murder of doubters and dissenters of established religions is still a fairly common occurrence in our enlightened and civilized world of programmed automatons.

Christianity re-enforces one of the great self-deceptions of mankind by telling us that man, unlike the animals, has been given a free will to choose either good or evil, and that man may do whatever his "conscience" dictates. But conscience is a product of programming, which limits and guides our every thought and action; our decisions, and subsequent performance are all results of our programming. We cannot be compassionate and caring, if we've been raised in violence and calloused by brutality. We cannot decide to play Beethoven's fifth symphony on the piano unless we have been programmed to play the piano, and not even then, unless we have been programmed in that particular composition.

We're more complex than the animals, but have many traits in common: Emotionally, we "feel" as a result of our thoughts. We think as we've been programmed to think, and our actions reflect our programmed thinking. This makes our every decision, our every deed, the result of the bias within the accumulated sub-total of our lives. The messages we've received have determined our path. Whether our programming leads us into drugs and an irrevocable maze of addiction - where past and future programming is ineffectual - or whether it forms the foundation of further knowledge, depends on the quality and truth of our early exposure.

From early beginnings man has lived a dual role. He has of necessity been a ruthless, unscrupulous pursuer of survival, while at the same time acting out the appeasement of a conscience synonymous with his programmed conception of a demanding God. He has corroborated, compared, and exaggerated his fantasies, fears, and dreams, until they have been given the credibility of established sources of knowledge. But unfortunately, corroboration of like thoughts by two or more of the same persuasion does not necessarily make a truth. The entire world is now largely programmed toward believing in the spirituality of man, and therefore massively biased toward validating the concept.

We have recently been in the process of collecting donations in the West to send fifty million bibles to the peoples of the USSR, who - after some seventy years of enforced atheism - have had their imagination fired by memory and opportunity to suddenly feel spiritually disenfranchised. Glasnos and Perestroika have created a void in leadership at a time when deprivation and a sense of loss present fertile ground for a religious revival - or even a return to communism. Gorbachev - the man who uncorked the vessel of state control and so inadvertently released the genie of religion along with all the other little "freedoms" that would hopefully lead to the productivity of individual endeavor - has now been politically defrocked because of Russia's ineffectual national recovery.

Gorbachev failed to anticipate the crippling of initiative that would result from prolonged programming of dependency on the State. The masses were paralyzed with chronic dependency created by government ownership, control, and patronage. Instead of emerging from beneath the yoke of state control with new incentive and individual drive, the people came forth to be emancipated in the abject misery of near starvation, substituting their reliance on the state for the crutch offered by the church. The reason was that - as in all deliberate and manipulative programming - the Soviet people had long been denied the broadening experience of alternate thought and contact.

Implanting the young

We bend the twig to shape the tree, and the earlier we start in on opinionated programming, the more irrevocable the distortion. Even before the age of three, a parent can inculcate a child with undesirable behavioral patterns, inexplicably inhibited behavior, and exaggerated and illogical phobias and fears. Parental example will also imprint undesirable habits such as violence, over-eating, smoking, drinking, persistent arguing, prolonged periods of sulking, spouse-abuse, or whatever. We program our children with habit and inhibition by presenting a transparent portrayal of our own inadequacies and failings. If only we ourselves were without the mental hooks of flawed behavior and opinion, we'd make better role models. In truth, each of us in our time has received wrong messages.

Brain-washing and programming of opinion within the human mind are insidious influences that leave the most intelligent recipient unaware of its intrusion and unconscious bias upon their subsequently learned truths. Hence renowned scientists - physicists, physiologists, anthropologists, paleontologists, biologists, or whatever - sometimes illogically try to reconcile their findings in later life with their earlier programmed religious beliefs. But there are other times and conditions, after the age of reason has been reached, that present fertile planting ground for these insidious hooks.

Protecting the implants

The more established religions are content to plant the hook in the mind of the child and reenforce by repetition, knowing that it will grow into a ring in the nose of the adult. The Catholic religion is so anxious to protect their implanted ideas from outside influence, that the establishment teaches the placing of guarding barriers around their programmed children by sending them to Catholic Schools and Catholic Hospitals where they'll only receive re-enforcement. There is no tolerance for an opposing religious or secular viewpoint, and otherwise intelligent people are prohibited from extraneous religious discussion unless they have sacerdotal representation. Catholic programming goes so deep that the chances of a programmed Catholic ever breaking free is more remote than in any other religion. Even if the subject could be persuaded to seriously listen to alternate thought, it would take many months, even years, of one-on-one de-programming, and even then he wouldn't be completely free of his religious inhibitions.

Nurturing the implants

The power of prayer is psychologically enhanced by social participation and posture. A thousand Moslems kneeling with foreheads pressed to the dirt is an awe-inspiring sight that sweeps away individualism, inhibiting the incidence of doubt or rejection. The very plurality of numbers presents a tide of opinion that intimidates the individual, coerces a like behavior, and demands total submission and acceptance.

Every religion in the world uses mass ritual for the same reason, using pleasantries such as community singing, flowers, fellowship, and loving remembrances that no one can take exception to. The church's extra-curricular duties, such as funerals, weddings and christenings, firmly implant a need for its presence within a community. All participatory rituals of a religion are clothed in emotion, for emotion is the stuff of which religious fanatics are made. The "sack cloth and ashes" syndrome manifests itself in the masochistic religious exhibition of the individual: Seventh Day Adventists stand on street corners in inclement weathers begging for pneumonia. The Jew, dressed like a medieval undertaker, stands rocking before the wailing wall to emphasize his prayer. The rheumatic nun prostrates herself, belly down and arms akimbo on a cold concrete floor. The Muslim abuses his knee joints by kneeling toward Mecca, and Buddhist monks have been known to make themselves into human torches by immersing their robes in gasolene and setting themselves on fire - in public places of course. All are victims of irrevocable programming, but at least Buddhists strive for a state of Nirvana in the real world by exuding love and compassion to all and sundry.

Religious and Political Opportunism

Both religion and politics deal with the beliefs of man. They are different issues inextricably married in bias, with each coloring the integrity of the other. The argument that the one deals with a believed life hereafter - the saving of the soul - and the other with the "here and now," is a bid for impartiality and segregation, but does not negate the fact that both influence - or rather seek to control - our earthly existence. Organized religion and politics are both manifestations of the individual's drive to direct and control. Politics is purportedly a more organizational and objective discipline, while religion is more personal, persecutive and psychologically subjective, and should never be allowed to infiltrate politics with its zealous control. Because religion by definition has a following, there is a constant threat that the leaders will turn political and overstep their mandate which is to prepare wayward souls for the next world. A conscious misdirection of power to satisfy an ego could influence a political decision. Whether we realize it or not, politicians and priests vie for control.

Different ideologies, religions, and political beliefs, will exist even in the face of an imposed secular political unity - as evidenced by the revised ideology and the rebirth of Christianity in Russia, after seventy years of imposed atheistic Communism. While the Western Powers view the break up of the Soviet Union Empire as a matter of re-alignment of allies, the Stato Della Citta Del Vaticano - the smallest, richest, and most opportunistic and politically aggressive state in the world - sees the vast, heavily populated areas of East Berlin, Poland, Czechoslovakia, Hungary, Romania, Bulgaria, and the Baltic States, as a potentially liberated source of revenue. The Pope has already made his "religious pilgrimages," winning the hearts, minds and purse strings of those seeking assurance; and those who have lost state patronage, or are programmed with memories of their early teachings, all need re-assurance for re-establishment!

The decision makers within the Catholic Church have in the past greatly increased their congregation with the edict that children of Catholic parents/parent must be given the "advantage" of Catholic teaching. An easing of their stance on birth control or abortion would greatly lessen the impact of this successful doctrine, and diminish their congregation.

An appeal for abstinence of sex is a denial that it is nature's essential driving force to procreate, yet that is the unrealistic approach being dictated by the Roman Catholic Church in preference to sanctioning the use of condoms - the only presently known method of lessening the odds of contracting

AIDS. The teachings of Humanae Vitae, (of human life) reaffirmed by Pope Paul VI in 1968, inhibited the common sense precautions of those who now have full blown AIDS. "The Roman pontiff can and ought to reconcile himself, and come to terms with progress, liberalism, and modern civilization." So sayeth the infallible Pope Pius IX!

Another harmful aspect of Catholicism is the virtual manufacture of spurious sins and sinners that creates a one-on-one clandestine relationship between the priest and his young followers. Catholicism centers on the natural sexual awakening of the young, and from the pulpit labels their known yearnings as "sinful lust," and "sins of the flesh." Having thus created "sinful behavior," the priest, by suggestion, guides the poor "sinners," one at a time, into his little, dark confessional box to purge and purify their souls by confessing their sexual fantasies and behaviors. Unless the priest is a eunuch, or the confessor utterly without sex appeal, the sexual arousal that follows becomes reciprocal and conspiratorial. And the longer the relationship, the more twisted and guilt-ridden both participants become. The confessor thinks he is guilty of being the instigator, but the chances are he's one of many victims caught in the same ritualistic snare.

For those with intelligence and a mind of their own, the Pope's intractable attitude is bringing scorn to the church instead of followers, and making pedophiles and homosexuals out of the vulnerable priests and their followers. Perhaps, with the weight of recent adverse publicity, the church will now - too late - relax its intransigence on priestly celibacy, and abandon the use of the little dark confessional box that renders the guilt-ridden prurient adolescent vulnerable to the sexually inhibited priest. It is these doctrines and practices that condone and reinforce aberrational behavior, together with repetitive forgiveness, absolution and renewal.

Flogging a dead horse

The age of communication is creating rebels within hitherto closed ranks, and for the first time in history the Pope travels world-wide in a political endeavor to rally ignorance and tradition. The result has little effect on an inexorable movement away from restrictive and ludicrously outdated trappings. The millions who flocked to see the Pope hoping for solutions, found only an intransigent man, imprisoned and impotent in the fervor of his beliefs, completely deaf to the problems of his followers in a changing, and economically hostile environment. He continued to demand adherence to an outdated dogma for fear that a change of stance by the church would cause loss of face, loss of piety for the church, weaken his personal power, and reduce congregation.

On every controversial issue that faces mankind, it is the militant, the fervent, the exhibitionists, or the ones with vested interests, who speak out to fight and sway public opinion. These vocal "special interest groups" create waves of bias that swamp the more circumspect silent majority, the uncommitted, the peace lovers, and the intelligent wimps. But by remaining silent and avoiding confrontation, this silent majority does more than condone the spread of falsehood and untruth. Silence is endorsement, not benign tolerance. It is time to take responsibility and demand accountability for pronouncements based on unsubstantiated opinion, for it is the messages that prevail that will decide the future of mankind.

Wisdom and tranquility will come to those willing to cease grasping for straws of hope in their subconscious quest to make the opinion of others their own personal truth. Life is infinitely more enjoyable without the inhibition of feeling on trial by an after-death tribunal. We free ourselves from a false sense of spirituality that arises from being thought chosen by an omnipotent God of our own imagination. Spirituality is a mental snare, set on the promise of corporeal divinity and man's immortality. It is the manifestation of our fear of death and the unknown. The reason we believe we are depleted for the lack of spirituality is this inherent promise of eternal life on another plane.

We are in fact depleted and limited by believing ourselves spiritually pre-ordained, and have little reason to believe we'd be anything but harassed and worn with an eternity of spiritual fulfillment and eternal bliss - a nebulous and even frightening prospect, considering the variety and depravity of man's pleasures of the flesh. Could we perhaps look forward to an eternity of orgasms, an eternal duplication of drug-induced euphoria, or alternately rocking on a porch in an indestructible chair?

When we are strong enough to turn to realism, we will gain an inner strength and independence in the knowledge that evolution has made us something more than the sum of our parts, miraculously complex, capable of challenging the secrets of immortality with our minds, and riding the universe like gods in our own right.

Religions have existed for as long as man's neuro-transmitters have been carrying messages that affect mood and behavior. Webster's definition of a religion is incomplete, in that it says what a religion is, but fails to say how religions are born. A definition of religion could be: "The successful development of a cult that advocates the concept of a god, by a leader seeking vicarious power by using mental seduction with coercive messages, reinforced by repetitive ritual, with the object of programming his followers to complete belief, submission, and assent. The longer a person practices religion, the less likely he is of ever breaking free'.

Less than five hundred years ago - about forty-four years after Columbus "discovered" America - the Catholic Bishops of England were instrumental in burning William Tynsdale at the stake for heresy. His "heresy" was the usurping of the Priest's vicarious power (their privileged knowledge of Latin) by smuggling his English translations of the New Testament from Germany to the common people of England - "so that they may read the written word of God" - supposedly captured in that holy book. The priests laid the onus for the death sentence on Henry VIII on the trumped up charge that Tynsdale, that remote and unconcerned man, was supposedly opposing Henry's divorce from Catherine of Aragon. He was just one of hundreds that suffered the same fate for the sole purpose of establishing firm control by the priesthood.

The chronically ill and suffering who believe death the eternal sleep of oblivion, welcome death without fear of consequence. However, if there is a God somewhere out in the cosmos who tinkers in human affairs, he must be a patient God, for he waited some four million years for the blossoming of the human brain before claiming credit as the creator just two millennium ago. This gargantuan creator sitting hunched like a cloud over a Chinese checker-board that is the universe has positioned the little blue marble that is the earth in a manner vital to the creation of life; one hole toward the red marble, and we'd fry, one hole back and we'd freeze! Among a trillion trillion stars and planets, those capable of supporting life are as scarce as police in a crime zone. And in a creation where man is - by his own assessment - of such importance as to be a replica of the creator himself, such an abundance of unusable real estate seems an awful waste!

Man's goal must be of this world, based on knowledge not opinion or blind faith. There must be change in our perception of what we are, not only to avoid inner conflict, continued wars, massacres, and possible total annihilation, but to release us from the limitation of believing our future pre-ordained. For in believing that our natural life span is at the discretion of another, our psyche will continue to accept the inevitability of a short and limited life - a fact that is becoming increasingly questionable in light of a present research that demonstrates that our life span, when discounting the equation of chance, circumstance and environment, depends on the programmed limitations within our DNA. Surely a more realistic goal would be the breaking of this restrictive formula and the attainment of a prolonged life, a life with universal quality, without the fear of death. A conquest of life over inert matter. The miracle and majesty of human life is in its potential for intelligence.

Mankind has clawed its way out of the primordial mud to rest on an evolutionary mountain top. We are metaphorically standing, wondering where next to go. There seems little purpose in our arrival. We've taken so long to get here, that the struggle itself has become our ultimate purpose. And that is exactly what it is. We've come a long way, and - in comparing ourselves to the animals - mistakenly imagine ourselves as a finished product, at the end of our evolutionary development.

Perhaps we still have as far to go as the survival of the species will permit. Only in very recent times have we reached a development that permits us to become participants in what amounts to an entirely new ball game. With our future active participation, life will become an exciting personal adventure. We can actually have an impact on our own destiny. Let us hope that restraint and wisdom in using our new found powers will circumvent, rather than cause, the destruction of our habitat and the end of life.

Sociologically we are still far behind our technological development, and as the pace of evolutionary change quickens with technology teetering on the brink of a biochemical marriage, we will realize that our headlong progress over the last hundred years was just the beginning of an exploding awareness of our true potential.

—The idea of human spirituality, an ever-present inner-self, a ghost capable of traveling after death, is beyond living authentication. It is a viral idea with a block end, persisting by virtue of the fact that death is an impenetrable oblivion.

Chapter 9

How a better balanced society is leading to anarchy

The suffragettes were a stridulent lot, but they succeeded in taking women out of the home and getting them terrible jobs in offices, hospitals, and schools. The majority of women became transcribers of the boss's thoughts and edicts, while sitting behind the lowly typewriter. A few managed to infiltrate the ranks of the professionals, but most occupied dead-end jobs, fondly believing themselves "emancipated." Webster's Collegiate Dictionary defines emancipation as "being freed from bondage," but, when used in connection with the status of women, it has come to mean the dubious accolade of being equated with men. However, at that stage, the majority became society's patsies for soul-destroying labor: bedpans and vomit, chalk dust and squalling kids, and prime candidates for carpal tunnel syndrome. Far better to be kept and closeted.

In this context, the greatest boost for the emancipation of women arrived very recently in the form of a new technology. For, while being inextricably married to a hunk of metal containing the alphabet, and being limited to transferring the boss's mundane thoughts to hard copy - which proved to be a boring, thankless, and dead-end job - they were in effect being programmed with an understanding of the business world. It was a serendipitous education that would lay dormant, waiting to meet up with opportunity in the form of a new technology.

The equalizing of opportunities came not so much through the presumptuous ambition of the typist, as through a transformation of the hunk of metal she used to transcribe. It turned out that the lowly typewriter had a brilliant future. Almost overnight, it blossomed into what was to become the beating heart of every limited company struggling to become a separate identity in perpetuity; it metamorphosed into an organizing masterpiece known as a word-processor-come-computer, with a memory bank and all the attachments and programs required to make a commercial, industrial, and professional revolution. The computer has literally changed the balance, and direction of society.

The new technology created a revolution that made accountants scramble in search of providing new services such as labor-placement agencies, business consultants, and income tax specialists. Companies were buying cheap accounting software packages that replaced the tediousness of accounting. Stock clerks, filing clerks, accounts payable clerks and accounts receivable clerks, either became redundant or computerized within their limited spheres of operation. But most of all, it elevated secretaries to the lofty positions of all-knowing oracles within the business world; and not just secretaries. The outgoing correspondence of business executives seeking to make a fast buck, were pearls of wisdom retained in memory to serve and to educate those unfortunates confined to typing pools. Computers became the status symbols of the modern office, and tens of thousands of typists in every kind of company throughout the business world had their obsolete typewriters replaced by computers with memory banks that provided an entree into the inner sanctum of business. An army of potential female executives was thus created almost overnight, to wait on the sidelines to take their turn at wheeling and dealing.

Computers became the filing systems, fountains of knowledge from which the boss sought information, and the computer operator - nee the typist - was in a position to extract and interpret this information at the touch of a button. (or several buttons!) The typist knew the business better than the boss. She knew enough to legally limit her liability and go into business for herself. What did she have to lose? Absolutely nothing!

Women witnessed how many of their number had suffered unwanted repetitive pregnancies, with all the accompanying economic miseries, and determined that they would avoid becoming victims of this barefoot and pregnant syndrome. They rushed into the void created by new opportunities. The lady had a brain, and she had the pill, and if she "slipped up," well - society was now looking more kindly on abortion. She even had medication to level out the emotional cycle of her menstrual period. She was practically a man - or so the front-line radical feminists wanted to believe - and the cold job-eligibility war between competing individuals expanded to include women. Some still retained their age-old weapon of sex and the withholding of same, but were now in a more independent position to use it.

Since time immemorial, big strong man had condescendingly reserved a place by the fire and a seat in the kitchen for the "little woman." Now he was being educated by circumstances to realize the true female potential. Why he should need such educating is a reflection on the strength of conventional, opinionated programming within the societies of the world. The lady was going out to work, and sometimes earning more than he was, and, in order to save the family unit - which is the operating base for the capitalistic system - he was finding himself sharing unbelievable chores that had menial overtones. Under the facade of "honoring and obeying" and accepting her allotted role, many wives had for some decades been usurping the easy going authority of the somewhat dozy male, to become the unofficial, unrecognized family decision-maker. Subtlety was never man's strong point. It was a case of, "Give me your wage-packet, honey, and go out and play baseball with the kids while I cook dinner."

Universities began to look at the female labor minority for academic qualifications and production potential, rather than allotting a patronizing quota of students in order to forestall any charges of discrimination. Women were beginning to be financially independent even with a less than equitable remuneration, and their lower wage structure was the incentive for pecuniary-minded employers to participate in the beginnings of a labor revolution.

Equal pay for equal service has been misrepresented and distorted to mean something quite different from that obviously laudable sentiment. Usually, the point of contention has been that one job performed by a woman can be equated to an entirely different job performed by a man. i.e., the girl in the cafeteria, standing and walking eight hours a day could be equated with the postman who also stands and walks eight hours a day. In other words, one or two aspects of two entirely different jobs have been used as a basis for equating them, and such cases adjudicated by a commission or panel of so-called "experts" who've had no realistic conception of what was involved, or little or no rationale for the issuance of their subsequent directive for equal pay. This form of equalization persists even today, and will inevitably create another damaging backlash.

The pundits on the panel sit and pontificate, and receive excellent compensation for forcing what might be a marginal operation into bankruptcy or voluntary closure, with the resulting unemployment of the griever. Such cases have been instigated by militant feminists, but the winning of these issues do little to enhance their cause, and contribute to an ongoing inequity in compensation. The vast silent majority of women are incensed that a militant few should presume to speak for the majority, with the result that other more conservative groups like "real women" are now speaking out.

Today, many working women no longer have to stay tied and subservient to loud-mouthed, chauvinistic boors with muscles; women are flocking into the professions, into politics, and into the power structure of commerce. They are becoming judges. They're on parole boards, juries, school boards, and hospital boards. They serve as ministers of the crown, congress women, take on ambassadorial duties, and even become prime ministers. India, Pakistan, Israel, and Great Britain have all benefitted from having female leaders.

President Bush had made wiser moves than when he sent an ambassadress to socially-backward Iraq where the prejudice against women is unconscionable. Sadam Hussein still thinks of women as chattels, and supports the veiling and herding of them in black shrouded groups. It is not a case of protecting women from licentious men. It is a form of control that smothers personality, denies individuality, and reduces women to a faceless common denominator. It is an exercise in intimidation and suppression, and though excused as a custom of the country, it never-the-less stunts the natural development of personality. In such an environment, any female envoy would have a difficult time commanding her due respect.

The western economy has now adjusted itself to an income level of minimal adequacy for a family with two working parents. A complete family unit living off the income of a single parent is now even worse off than the single working parent. The age-old institution of marriage, with the dutiful little woman working in the home, has developed a flaw. Money worries and quarrels drive the somewhat confused and financially strapped male out to find comfort with the free and easy, financially independent working girl. The western world has made it easier to get divorces, so why not get them? Single parentage is now socially acceptable if still economically difficult. But pragmatic governments have brought child-care facilities on line, and hold delinquent alimony payers to account. And so the impediment against separation is removed, and the divorce rate has shot up.

The reciprocal and tacit agreement between man and woman that existed since the beginnings of time, whereby the man served as provider and protector in exchange for sex, love and the privilege of producing little self-replicas, is threatened, if not null and void. At last men are listening to women, and in order to save a way of life, they have no option but to become more tolerant and flexible toward their now "equal," and often unmarried, partners.

Today, the radical feminists are so encouraged by their new found independence, that they are unrealistically denying the basic, fundamental biological differences between the sexes; differences in brain, frame and muscular build, mental and emotional processes, drive, reaction, sensitivity, illness susceptibility, learning abilities, temperament - obvious differences, long acknowledged by researchers, both female-biased, and impartial. It is because of these undeniable differences that the concept of totally equating the sexes is inappropriate, and will in time revert to an acknowledgment that we are essentially different, each with attributes and disadvantages, but neither superior. And as Maurice Chevalier once quipped "Viva la difference!"

It is true that certain "butch" women are wrestlers, boxers, undercover police women, and - given the chance - army fighting machines. These women, like effeminate men, will always be the exceptions. By and large, the female of the species is more sensitive, more compassionate and more patient than the male, who evolved as the fighter, hunter and provider. And this is where the trouble starts.

The increasing influence of the gentler sex on society has brought about profound changes in diluting harsh punishment and discipline. For decades, we've been entering a period of permissiveness that is sending out messages too complex, too obtuse for a society guided by the more direct and simpler forms of deterrents; punitive deterrents that were easily understood and heeded by the criminal element - who are mostly men.

If a small child is disobedient and throws a tantrum, a pat on the bum is now construed as child abuse rather than necessary discipline. We must reason with children who border on the vicious, and we are impotent in doling out suitable punishment for the worst criminal offenders, brutal murderers, and rapists. Schools have all but given up trying to discipline children who smoke, drink and trade in drugs. Capital punishment, as a response to serial killings, is now considered by a majority as inhumane, making us no better than the murderers. Perhaps psychoanalysis and rehabilitation are not such bad ideas. Prisons are stark, cruel places, more fit for animals; we must make them more comfortable with television sets, radios, and even sun rooms. The age of leniency began three or four decades ago, and is still maintained, on the premise that violence only begets violence, and cruelty begets cruelty. President Bush, in his inaugural speech, once again endorsed greater tolerance, saying, "Let us be a kinder, and gentler America." The message was taken out of context and misunderstood. We have been kind to the point of showing tolerance through leniency for the most atrocious of crimes. Permissiveness has spread to every level of society.

Breadwinners abandon children and spouses to the social workers and the tax payers. Embezzlement is on a grand scale, and vicious crime at every level is rampant. Society has become plagued with murderers, rapists, arsonists, and incorrigible pedophiles who, because of their early programming, cannot be easily rehabilitated. Today, a pedophile fears only public exposure, and the abuse of other criminals with whom he may be incarcerated. Rapists and pedophiles cannot be treated leniently, even if they were under the influence of drugs or alcohol at the time. Pedophiles cannot be relocated in the hope that they will change their behavior. Irrespective of programming or circumstances, we cannot accept mitigating excuses for such crimes against the sanctity of innocent people. We are sending out wrong messages, and there will inevitably be a backlash of harsher measures.

Murderers often crave public notoriety, and add to their infamy by serial killing. To those who lived through the tranquility before the "gentler age came about," the world has become a mad place. We try to blame it all on the judges, the Mafia, or the police, whereas society itself is at fault for prematurely adopting "go soft" policies before even attempting to sternly address the problem of re-programming aberrant behavior. It is not being humane, sensitive, or understanding, to condone violence of any kind by giving trivial sentences for heinous crimes. The message must be there for those with like propensities, even if it is tempered with appropriate psychiatric treatment and punitive re-programming for the perpetrator.

Even police forces and politicians, those once stalwart pillars of integrity, have become discouraged by the response of the courts, and have in many towns deteriorated into an opportunistic and cynical rabble that seek only to line their own pockets. When government, judicial and penal systems lose the respect and the control of the masses, we are indeed heading for anarchy.

In the relationship between man and woman, one partner cannot assume more power and responsibility without the other relinquishing it. Evolution made the male the fighter, the father, the provider, and the unilateral decision-maker, until five seconds ago on the evolutionary clock when he became all but redundant. Now, unless his country is at war, or he's fighting his wife over the decision-making process, he's a superfluous one-legged duck, unable to even discipline his own children without fear of interfering government agencies.

The function to "provide" is now a shared task, sometimes entailing looking after the children or doing household chores, while the spouse brings home the bacon. Unfortunately decision-making can't be shared, not even by a committee. Members can discuss, take a vote, reach a consensus, and even arrive at a conclusion. But members cannot make unilateral decisions. With two people there is no deciding majority, and differing marital decision-making calls for either undemocratic capitulation, unacceptable bullying, or a more acceptable bargaining process.

With the introduction of sperm banks, petri dishes and paid donors, the male is no longer even necessary as the father. And so, while the female is forging ahead, elevating herself in purpose and function, becoming an amazon in the business of living, the male is left with an ambivalence of purpose, confused, and kicking the dust.

Purpose to life

To pre-suppose purpose to life is to insinuate a master-plan, or a grand manipulator with intent. Both Sigmund

Freud and Carl Jung spoke of sex and the pursuit of happiness as major driving forces in our lives, but happiness is a mental response to a gratifying circumstance, and is a mere spray of chemical across the receptors of the mind. Is this then our purpose? Are we to be equated with laboratory rats that press buttons for rewards? Perhaps that is a true analogy, for after the fulfillment of basic needs, we continually pursue conducive and pleasing circumstances, like drug addicts seeking a shot of euphoria or instant gratification.

Needs are the essential incentives to life, but - without wishing to trivialize life - "wants" are just as important, for they provide the reasons for living for the first three quarters of our lives. When we cease to want things - an image, self-esteem, holidays, cars, and boats etc - we are literally losing our zest for life. And we call this blind pursuit of want "ambition." Some never get the satisfaction of achieving more than a level of need, and give up, to seek their satisfaction out of a bottle, while others resort to the needle. Even those who have everything want something more; it is the nature of man.

We like to credit our existence with a greater purpose than nature's edict that we live long enough to procreate before death. We've become more than the flowers, and must have a more profound destiny than the pursuit of sexual gratification as a purpose for living. As individuals, our only commonality is our drive to survive and make our mark. Some seek fulfillment in "creating" - painting, writing, sculpturing, making jewelry, and other kinds of self-gratification. Others seek short term goals throughout their lives, and achieving them provides a shallow but ongoing reason for living. However, the wish for "ultimate purpose," some earth shattering consequence that will imbue our lives with importance, is the self-made emptiness within us all. Our egos won't permit of a concept that places us on earth through mere chance and natural mutation.

The anatomy of the human body, from its outer skin to its inner heart, expresses purpose - as does every part of every living thing - but it is the purpose of functionability to survive as a whole, and merely demonstrates the evolutionary adaptation to need, and to a particular environment. The brain itself has an overriding purpose to use its programming to one end - survival. Everything we do, every act, is in some way - directly, indirectly, or remotely - connected to our need to survive.

Each one of us is in effect a vehicle by which the cells make the organs that serve the body, producing a cell-serving intelligence to prolong life. The very diversity of living matter illustrates the natural process of cell symbiosis, the struggle of the individual cell to fuse with others in a habitat that prolongs its life by an interacting process. This is the nature of all life, including disease that threatens life - for disease is a parasitical life form that seeks to live and multiply in our bodies, in competition with our protective immune systems. In a larger sense we are also parasites, living off of plants, or animals that have eaten plants.

Those with religious leanings credit their existence with a "divine" purpose, reasoning that their existence is a contribution to God's ultimate purpose. In our conceptual degree of importance, to be such a tool with a purpose is judged to be of a higher use than leading an aimless life. But with or without that belief, each of us is unique in both form and thought, for the chance permutation and diversification of experience gives us creativity through a pollination of thought, and - within the parameters of our programming, which can be expanded with the programming of ambition - a choice to set our own goals.

There is no single item or entity in nature that can claim "ultimate purpose." If there were, it would be incontrovertible evidence of the presence of a Supreme Being. A tree ends up as a log on the fire, fulfilling man's purpose to keep warm. A chicken crosses the road, and ends up on the dinner table, fulfilling his need to eat. Everything in nature interacts, creating contrast and opportunity by chance, not purpose. Whether we perceive ourselves as being self-actuated, or string-pulled marionettes, with some god awaiting proof that our "souls" are worthy of entry into Paradise, is the difference between reaching for a final goal within our lifetime or preparing for a mythical Utopia after death.

The human race is indeed reaching for something beyond its collective lifetime. Ever since we built a fire to provide warmth, we have become aware of our potential to beat nature by controlling it. We followed up this achievement by discovering clothing, cloth weaving, boats, animal husbandry, agriculture, ships, automobiles, electricity, plumbing and plastics; practically every acceptable advancement could be said to have the common and viable purpose of beating nature's harsh environment, shoe-horning life, and placating the frustrated animal within us. Consciously, or unconsciously we are striving to make life on earth - or life in the universe we hope to eventually conquer - a factual heaven for our descendants. We will certainly not reap the ultimate benefits of Homo sapiens progress within our own short lifetime, even though it may somewhat cushion the remainder of our short lives.

The competition to protect and propagate our bloodline is the human equivalent of the tom-cat killing a mother's kittens so that he may impregnate her with his own bloodline. And though individualism again rears its head to ensure the continuance of a particular blood line, our collective preparation is for a lifestyle that accrues for our respective descendants. We might argue with some truth that our purpose in improving a lifestyle for unborn generations is more of a by-product of our own egoism than a conscious act of altruism.

Raising standards

We continue to build onto a lifestyle that is already vastly superior to anything that any earthly animal has ever experienced, and we are more concerned with the prolongation of life of our direct descendants, than helping those of the third world. For, unless it leaves our present lifestyle untouched, the sharing of our level of comfort with those of the third world is definitely not in the cards.

CHAPTER 10

An Off-Shoot of Homo Sapiens?

Though society is stratified along many different levels, there is an insidious division taking place that is a separation of the active and the passive, the participating and the non-participating.

Our growing numbers of aged have witnessed a third generation being born on the crest of a technological revolution. It has carried them ahead into the future, and given rise to a need to send new messages, retool industry, retrain labor, and revise concepts of qualifications. It has created obsolescence and redundancies, and widened generation gaps to separate and disenfranchise a preponderance of the aged with a sense of being divorced from the mainstream of society.

But more than that, this new technology is creating an exclusion of participation for certain areas of human intelligence; a division that cuts through the populace, segregating non-compatible intelligence of all ages, interest and occupation:

within the younger generation, the elderly, between intellectuals, entrepreneurs, and even the average working man. Further, a specialized elite intelligentsia, backed by some governments, or the private funding of the fabulously wealthy, is keeping the hedonistic masses content and occupied with the commercialized toys and trivialities that keep the economy turning. Taxation and private funding pay for the more serious business of continued research into the marriage of biology and technology, the prolongation of life, the curing of gerontological disease, and the penetration and understanding of the cosmos; areas of research and development in which the average person will never participate, and never see any benefit other than the commercialized by-products.

The widening gap between the lower/middle classes and the affluent is already reflected in the flow of money around the world, with the middle classes being virtually eliminated. Eighteen percent of the 250,000000 population in the U.S.A. took home more income in 1994, than the whole of the remaining eighty-two percent. Similar inequities are occurring in Britain,

Germany, France, Japan, and even in Russia and Poland. For some unexplained reason we are witnessing a growing financial cleft that is related to the social gap between where the wealth already resides, and the middle and lower classes.

An intellectual elite, set apart with the genes of understanding, and programmed with the pure sciences, perhaps more advanced along the evolutionary road, are really worth the government sponsoring, for we lesser mortals seem abysmally lacking in comparison. Payment for lifestyle detracts from the reality that we are traveling on the coat tails of a superior intelligent minority.

Many of us take a plane without knowing what keeps tonnage elevated and flying. We listen to the radio, or watch TV, with only a vague appreciation that sound and vision are being somehow snatched from the air. We drive a car, knowing only that it has a combustion engine that consumes gas and oil, and requires new tires every couple of years. Perhaps ninety percent of the population of North America wear wrist-watches, and consult this essential gadget as many as two thousand times in a year, but to find anyone who could succinctly explain how this regulator of his life maintains a consistent measurement of time throughout its waning life span, (whether spring or battery) would be like looking for the proverbial needle in a haystack. The electronic computer is "user friendly," which is to say that its intelligence accommodates the stupidity of the user, but further, the computer seduces its users to neglect the learning of their own educational basics. The VCR was judged too complicated for the masses, and has now been re-engineered to self-adjust for timing and programming. And so the accommodation of ignorance continues, to nurture further lethargy, indifference and ignorance.

The changing world is preoccupying and seducing us with the conveniences and pleasures of a benign lifestyle that requires no understanding. As in our early beginnings, we are again living with a simplistic appreciation of much we don't understand, a partial cognizance of increasingly sophisticated stimuli that we can enjoy, see, hear, and experience without understanding. We are being entertained without realizing that we are also being seduced and alienated from the reality of participation, for without understanding of the things we've come to rely on, we live in a world of perceived pseudo magic. The result can only be the development of a passive, entertainment-craving mentality rather than an active, curious and aggressive one that seeks out the why and the how; the former leads to fatalism and acceptance without challenge, the latter leads to individual involvement and incremental growth - diverging paths that lead to opposite sides of a widening chasm. And we justify our non-participation by protesting that we can't be experts in everything. Life's becoming too complicated! Which is true for too many!!

We are becoming accustomed to hearing about major air disasters, and we accept tube explanations. The earth warming and hot-house effect. The breakdown of our ozone layer. The massive pollution. We accept the outrageous TV repair bill, or the garage repair bill. We accept because we're in no position to protest or dispute. We are non-participants in an evolving complexity. We are ignorant! And ignorance is an accumulating fact of life in a society that becomes more computerized, more complicated, more obtuse and devious, with every passing day.

Notwithstanding the reality of specialization among the trained technicians who service our toys, technicians are equally ignorant in matters outside of their specialized spheres of expertise. For the average mentality, the very volume of ongoing new technology demands specialization. Between those in the upper echelon of intelligence - those who understand Einstein's Theory of Relativity without any great difficulty, and those who think it a load of hog-wash - there is a growing chasm that has little to do with formal education. The really "gifted" benefit little from channeled education. They decide their own speed and level of advancement. Nothing can stop their participation. Their genius is not diluted with integration, but puddles in common interests, inherited genes, compatible marriages and programming. Each generation of the involved and comprehending moves further ahead, while the uninvolved and ignorant fall further behind.

On a lower level still, are those moronic individuals with closed minds and massive egos who program opinion without foundation in their offspring. We don't have to travel to the far corners of the earth to find a primitive tribe that still believes the earth to be flat. We still have among us such people as are in the Flat Earth Society! One lady who should be a chartered member, has convinced her children and her neolithic husband that the televised moon landing was a propaganda stunt devised to intimidate the Russians. She stoutly suggests that Hollywood can fake anything, and maintains this viewpoint in the face of world-wide acknowledgment to the contrary, because she saw the American moon-flag move with the wind. And of course she's been told that there isn't any wind on the moon!

Though the least of us have a potential a thousand-fold more than we realize or use, some never relinquish or modify their entrenched beliefs, and consider it their duty to stultify their children and their children's children with their absurd and illogical programming. With such dead-end thinking there can only be a parting of the ways between obdurateness and open-mindedness. Ideas can be mental blocks passed from one generation to the next, and in time the obdurate can only remain "stuck in the mud," while those who already belong to the intelligentsia, in reaching for knowledge and recognition, will literally reach the stars, for when they fully understand the science of genetic engineering, they will surely use it to further enhance their own potential. Within a comparatively short time their increased level of science could likely create a completely different species, an advanced off-shoot of Homo sapiens.

Perspective

We are not conscious of ongoing evolutionary change. Just as there are sounds beyond our range of hearing and micro-organisms beyond our range of sight, the concept of evolutionary change within our species - over aeons of time, involving thousands of generations - is beyond our empirical experience or imagination, and only recently proven by archaeological findings.

However, the evidence of natural selection is all around us if we care to look. We know that Pygmies don't live in jungles because they're small. They're small because they live in jungles and have adapted to travel through heavy undergrowth. We know that black men are not black because they're inferior. They're black because they have adapted to hot climes where a dark pigment gives them more protection. Ducks have webbed feet because they have adapted to paddling along in water. The Arctic tern has a wing configuration that allows it to fly twenty-two thousand miles in its yearly quest for greener pastures. Every species around us has unique adaptations that enhance its chance of survival.

In a recent book entitled *The Beak of the Finch,* the author cites the observations by a scientist named Grant, who claimed that over a twenty year period, while staying on an island called Daphne Major, he actually witnessed proof-in-action of Darwin's evolutionary theory of natural selection. Apparently drought killed off a flock of finches, except those with beaks capable of cracking the harder nuts. Subsequent generations therefore had larger beaks, until a flood of "almost biblical proportion" created small soft nuts that could only be eaten by those with small beaks.

Whereupon the survivors had offspring with small beaks. In an evolutionary sense it is still the message that determines our future.

To a creature with a life span of a mere three score and ten, a hundred and fifty years seems a long time. But in an evolutionary sense where time stretches back in infinity, this last century has been the cutting edge of man's development, changing the average Homo sapiens from a rural bumpkin - unaware of his ignorance and confined to his village and its gossip - to a knowledgeable cosmopolitan. He is a product of the information age, perhaps flawed and biased, but with a new found awareness and understanding that carries him still further away from other living creatures.

However, as individuals, we might ask ourselves, "how much of me is really me?" Sound ridiculous? Perhaps not. To put it another way - how much of you is the product of another's programming, and how much is the product of your own shaping? Remember earlier on in the book we said we are all to some extent behaviorally programmed, to some extent mind-poisoned by example, to some degree manipulated? Well, examine your lifestyle, your daily routine, your addictions, habits, your circle of friends and acquaintances. If you smoke, drink alcohol, or take drugs, you certainly didn't program yourself to it. Conscious self-programming is never injurious to one's self. Someone else did it to you either by example or coercion. If you sulk, fly into a tantrum, or cry without apparent reason, someone else did it to you. No one programs himself to unhappiness. But it's never too late to re-program yourself. It's just not easy.

Programming by another person is not always harmful of course. It can be most beneficial. King, the deceased black leader, said, "I have a vision," and that vision was equality for black people. A vision that certainly enhanced the equality they should have had centuries earlier. Conversely, harmful programming can be "built on" or an extension of another's harmful programming. Hate is an emotion passed on by deed or opinion. Dislike is a benign thought. It doesn't damage the psyche or health, but to sleep with hate is to be in bed with a viper. Programming evokes behavior and emotion. Hate programming creates aberrational behavior and violence.

The swiftness of recent changes around us has given us less security and a greater sense of our tenuous relationship with the world in which we live. Only in the last thirty years have we become aware of the need for a balanced ecology. Only in the last fifty-odd years have we realized that all matter is made from the same building blocks called atoms. Only in the last twenty-odd years have we realized that all living creatures have a DNA blueprint, and that we are comprised of living cells that can themselves send messages. Only in the last hundred years have we developed societal systems, electricity, and food distribution systems that could, with application and no political interference, circumvent localized famine. Only in the last forty years has the prolongation of life become a reality with the advent of human implants, or with the actual curing of disease. Only in the last fifty years, with the shadow of the nuclear bomb hanging over us, have we been compelled to stop and think before rushing into senseless war, for we are learning what we are, what are our needs, our options, and the viability of our route to the stars. For without challenge and progress we now realize that we will return to a state of stagnation, a state that we have endured for too long.

We are on the move, taking charge of our bodies, our environment, and our direction. Only over the last fifty years have we developed what could be called a world-wide net-working communication system that enables the world community to respond in unison to senseless aggression, and bring their combined discretionary powers to enforce diplomacy and restraint on those who would be military aggressors.

We have demonstrated the creation of primitive life forms, and created clones of some of the lower reptilian animals. We've witnessed the ability of some species to regrow lost limbs and tails. We've seen animals change color to camouflage themselves in the changing seasons and backgrounds. We've discovered fossil remains of every imaginable species, both living and extinct, that have crowded the earth. We have found dinosaur bones dating back some sixty-five millions years, when they were destroyed with most living things in the cataclysmic collision of a gigantic meteorite with earth.

And we have proven the evolutionary renewal process of symbiosis that resulted in new species that have evolved from the formation of different interrelated living organisms since that time. We understand the process that created an infinite variety of every conceivable creature - slithering, crawling, leaping, hopping, walking, no legged, two legged, four legged, six legged, eight legged, and even a hundred legged centipede. Just as plants reach for the light, and their roots reach for moisture, so do living cells seek continuance by a process of symbiosis. We are now supreme among the animals, and yet it wasn't always so. We are the most successful combination of living cells that has evolved since the dinosaur ruled the earth for a hundred and forty-five million years, its successful DNA perpetuating itself by propagation until its oblivion in the darkness of an obliterated sun.

We know that the life-span of the human individual, though infinitely important within the limited perspective of his existence, is but an insignificant speck of chalk dust on the evolutionary blackboard of life. And we realize that a successful attempt at the prolongation of life, though a major breakthrough, would in reality be confined to the favored few, and of little consequence, being merely limited prolongation. For, in the reality of the continuation of the species, those chosen would be no more than static dead-end branches off the evolutionary growth of the species, for an immortal, without evolutionary adaptation to change, would become an obsolete dinosaur, losing the pleasure of being a part of its own species. On the other hand, an elite intelligentsia could decide that Homo sapiens are taking up too much room, and utilizing too much of the earth's resources. A superior intelligence could very easily rectify that.

While the ingestion or injection of certain chemicals during a term of pregnancy can damage the DNA within the fetus and create a mutant, or major deformity in the child, whole societies, cultures, countries, and even land formations will inevitably change or disappear in the time it takes for the process of natural evolution to bring significant change to the human species. When we consider the evolutionary time it has taken to make us what we are, it is no wonder that we question our origin, and look for magic. For millions of years, we were unaware of the existence of our brain, much less being capable of questioning its function. And when we eventually became aware that we had an "inner driving force"- a decision-making process that gave us guidance - a part of our mind attributed it to a doting God steering us through life's awesome maze, giving us a "soul" on loan, that must be returned at the time of death - unless of course rejected as damaged and sent to hell!

For millions of years the brain remained undefined, unrecognized as our essence and initiator. For millions of years it developed and worked incognito. Thoughts became expressed in speech, betraying motives in thought, and so the brain censored vocalization and veiled itself with deceit and hypocrisy. Body language exposed emotions and intent, and, like the faces of poker players, became masked and controlled. For nothing must reveal the selfish intent, or interfere with the promotion of the self-image. Because the need for favorable recognition is the underlying incentive behind all ambition, research is shrouded, and all unsharable human endeavor is secret. There thus developed a complete inner self, quite different to the facade we show the world, or even our own spouse. Our thoughts represent the true brain, our speech the ventriloquist's dummy, saying and acting on the world stage.

The human brain, laying hidden in anonymity, and working vicariously, has become the strongest, most powerful force the world has ever seen. It is literally capable of moving mountains, changing the seas, or destroying all life. It is becoming the lord of all creation, with no science beyond its understanding, no challenge too large, no detail too small. Three hundred years ago we lived in villages, completely preoccupied with rural life. It would seem a contradiction that this sophisticated intelligence could develop over a mere three hundred years. But the pace of change will again undergo rapid acceleration when the marriage of human intelligence and technology produces chemical biotechnology.

We now live on the edge of profound evolutionary change that will have far reaching repercussions. While past evolutionary change has been as spectacular and as unobtrusive as the proverbial drying paint, the very requirements for the survival of the species are now swiftly changing around us, moving away from robust health and brute strength to the more subtle attributes of intelligence and the understanding of an increasingly complex technology. The delicate and the ailing are being elevated to make possible not only their survival, but the productive use of their abilities to play leading and contributing roles in the promotion of human affairs. If our species survives long enough, bodily systems might even now be changing to cope with increasing demands, pollution, a changing food chain and environment.

Changing circumstances and technologies are altering the relationship and balance between the sexes, with the male losing his dominance. In fact there is currently a very real danger that male children of today will be the impotent adults of tomorrow, due to the leaching out of estrogenic pollutions in the manufacture and common household uses of plastics that are largely responsible for our high standard of living. To avoid irreparable damage to future generations we need immediate government legislation demanding that all plastic manufacturers disclose the chemicals they use in the making of their different forms of plastic - currently considered “trade secrets.” Also, propyl alcohol is in practically every household product, and is a deadly catalyst in the cause of all cancers.

The individual feels comparatively safe in the bosom of society, but society itself is as fragile as the individual, and could be eliminated by epidemics or impotency within a single lifetime. It will take years before we see the detrimental effects of estrogenic pollution upon our children. Over the past three decades, it has permeated our oceans and rivers, affecting every living creature in the food chain, and it now becomes the responsibility of science, medicine and technology to combat these threatening substances to ensure the continuation of the species.

Half an idea that changed man’s development

As recently as only four thousand years ago, we were totally ignorant of our potential. Our simplistic lifestyle was our only opportunity for stimulus and self programming, and perhaps utilized five percent of our mental capacity. Whether by pre-birth programming or in the formative years, all animals teach their young how to survive, but only the human animal has realized the potential inherent in changing the behavior of its young.

Homo sapiens had instinctively been teaching survival tricks for millions of years to its offspring, but when someone - probably a father teaching his son these "tricks" - suddenly realized that he had the power to change his son in ways other than in hunting techniques, he happened upon an earth shattering revelation. He could gather information and pass it on to his son. It was a profound and far-reaching thought that amounted to a partial recognition of the very nature of mankind. The realization enabled man to concentrate his behavior in a more productive way. It enabled mankind to function more efficiently, and prevail to achieve our present level of technology.

Like most of our discoveries, it was merely one idea leading to another, but it was a breakthrough that changed the course of humanity and literally rocketed us into the modern world. For whoever that man was, he was the first to realize that in teaching his son, he was actually directing a change in the course of human behavior, to perhaps set it on an entirely different path. It was mind boggling! It was the birth of "directed" education - the one method that could set in motion an aimed programming process that was the basis of accumulative knowledge, a truth serum that produced selective investigative thinking. Seeing his son pass on the knowledge like regurgitated food to the grandson was the directed start of generation educating generation, first by example, then verbal communication, then in writing, film, radio, television, telecommunication, satellite, and every electronic marvel of the information age.

But even before knowledge was expressed in writing, it became quickly apparent that education gave people ideas that were not always in accord with those in authority. Ideas made people confrontational, causing dissension and even revolt. Education provided a weapon of knowledge that the priests, the potentates, and the privileged thought should be prudently confined to their own armory. Knowledge held the power to change a person's self-image, character, loyalty to a particular religion, and obedience to a higher authority. For education set knowledge against opinion, and was certainly not a suitable pursuit for the masses. Privileged scholars and priests began to confine the expression of their thoughts to Latin, and so exclude the average person. Independent thinkers were treated as heretics and burned at the stake. It was the beginning of four thousand years of suppression and mind control.

The twentieth-century brought the industrial revolution, which did more than just bring together a work force from all parts of the country. It brought together individuals of common interests; individuals who converged on industrial sites within cities, and generated ideas for their collective betterment, which was a form of street education and a certain conformity of opinion, not always in accord with the ruling elite. They coalesced into trade unions and societies. For individuals are opportunistic, and will join Unions, the Elks, the Free Masons, the Boy Scouts, or the Girl Guides, on the chance that it will provide liberation, opportunity, recognition, or financial gain. The more we know, the more we want to know, for when we program ourselves on knowledge, intelligence itself snowballs with understanding. Public education became a fact, which emancipated the ignorant and placed individuals in a common societal arena with plenty of ammunition for communication and confrontation.

The individual's relationship with Society

Adversity has been our evolutionary classroom, acceptance of instability our philosophy, and decision and confrontation our response. We are being transported through co-operative knowledge to the twenty-first century, from tribe to town to city to society, while still wearing our insecurity like a cloak. And society - being comprised of individuals - has assumed the confrontational attitude of the individual, to become the arena in which he confronts his alter ego. Every individual thrives on challenge, altercation and dispute; and every social contact, every business contract, every game and every sport, every considered alliance, and every plan of action, is a confrontational challenge - civilized perhaps but confrontational with obstacles to overcome. For without challenge, opposition and confrontation, we cease to be a force. We become impotent in the decision making process. Our drive to survive has become our reason for living. Society is the individual pluralized, and is just as ruthless, just as relentless, and just as unforgiving.

We as individuals rebel against society, (i.e.; another individual's ruling) and the way it makes us conform to traffic and pedestrian ordinance, to clock time and meal times, to lawful behavior, and internal organizational systems.

Society itself is a master system, controlling other internal systems, stratifying and categorizing individuals into laborers, office workers, tradesmen, professionals, and retirees. We fight to break from these molds as we fought to break from the womb, and as we fight for every level of Mazlow's hierarchy of needs. Labels inhibit and frustrate ambition and movement - unless we have attained one that coincides with our preconceived status, one that gives individual satisfaction and prestige in society's pecking order. We fight against circumstances that permit society to use derogatory labels. We fight against societal systems, and in the fighting we sometimes damage our own interests. One might deduce that we still have a long way to go toward developing a social conscience - which is merely saying we need to relinquish some "self interest" territory.

Society also provides an environment of confrontation, hardship and struggle that we understand, and to which we respond by becoming motivated - until we get old and unable to compete to the same degree. We deteriorate physically as individuals, and become resistant to change in the latter part of our lives, largely because change is a challenge with which we can no longer cope, whereas society constantly receives the renewal of youth to remain virile, impersonal, unrelenting and ruthless, in an ever-changing mode that gathers momentum to ride roughshod over the aged, and leap ahead to cause generation gaps. It is a process that fulfills nature's edict that the fittest shall survive, if only temporarily. It is a duplication and projection of our early beginnings, when age succumbed to the harshness of nature.

Unrealistic expectations of societal change

We have long recognized that organized co-operative endeavor can achieve more than individual effort, and this is the idealistic - but not always practical - basis upon which socialism is formed To have concerted effort, we must have equal universal collective motivation. We must have common goals, and unanimous agreement as to which route to take in order to achieve them. These are impossibly unrealistic expectations while individuals, with differing circumstances - wealth and aptitude, with differing needs and viewpoints, not to mention those with programming that has caused aberrational behavior - proliferate society. Without the necessary ground work to level the playing field - the programming of common fundamental truths, and the impossible leveling of human potential that requires individuality be reduced to that of a working cog in a machine - the concept of common societal endeavors, or societal accord, will always be on shaky ground, and only temporarily resolved by political majorities.

CHAPTER 11

Politics

The winds of change

Anyone who has seen the surge of motion caused by gusting winds through a field of prairie wheat, can imagine the impact of a satellite news system on the world population. The more efficient the transmission system, the faster the wave and impact on society. Overwhelming demand for a product can be created overnight. One sentence created a national binge on oat bran. Doctor Linus Pauling, two-time Nobel Prize winner, stated the opinion that vitamin C would cure the common cold - an erroneous opinion from a credible source - and every outlet in the Western world sold out of vitamin C in three days. Most successful politicians achieve their potential by using the mass media, and many use it to promote opinion as fact.

The ability to portray immediacy from one side of the world to the other creates painful revelations that highlight our vulnerability to programming. Instant national awareness creates explosive exposure and disclosure, shocking in impact to our naive perception of human decency. A blast of simultaneous national exposure creates false authentication as fact. It is a very different world to the insulated one that had time for psychological parameters of disbelief as a response to shocking human behavior.

In the last ten years we've witnessed the opening up of the homo-sexual closet, the disclosure that some forty percent of the Catholic Priesthood are homosexuals, the exposure that Catholicism has been a hide-out for child molesters, and that seemingly respectable pillars of society can turn a blind eye to behavior that denigrates us from the superior animals we like to think ourselves. The new technology has exposed the world to the magnitude of violent crimes, the ineffectual societal response, and the world-wide blatant corruption among politicians seeking to control development and be on the inside track to line their own pockets. The information age is holding a mirror to the human face, and it's not a very flattering reflection.

Individualism vs Systems

It is the nature of the individual to want to organize, expedite, and control, and so-called civilized societies under the direction of scheming and strategically placed politicians, resort to the use of systems to achieve this end. Politics are fraught with self-serving opinion and misleading messages. It is the goal of politicians to be on the winning side, or on the side with the financing that makes such political careers possible and worthwhile - which results in low or no taxes for the large supporting corporations, not always on the side of truth or the side of the humanitarian directive.

With growing and spreading populations, the age-old tribal hierarchical systems of control became remote and impersonal, or unwieldily and fragmented. Tribes became villages, and villages towns, and then cities. Citizenship became a privilege with amenities and attached costs and obligations. As populations grew, leaders began innovating by using artificial systems to extend their influence - systems that would give politicians vicarious power to organize, control, and expedite the lives of other individuals.

As the individual began to feel the increasing pressures of being subjected to controlling systems that demanded his active participation - Federal, State, and Municipal systems, judicial systems, income tax, purchase tax, welfare, health care, and ecological systems, not to mention the natural developing hierarchical systems of commerce and industry - his natural aversion to being directed and controlled resulted in his scheming to break out, or avoid the imposed obligation of paying his dues, while still reaping the benefits of an organized society. The tax systems that politicians institute and support, are often against the individualistic nature of those who find themselves manipulated and regulated. It is the exploited majority that usually pays, for a *pinch* from the impotent poor and middle class majority has less repercussion and equal results as a *grab* from the influential and rich minority. Consequently, the poor have no room to maneuver, and no recourse other than to try to cheat on tax structures that impose further poverty.

A political system should be a system devised to benefit society by organizing, directing and controlling with legislated laws. It must be seen to be fair, and above suspicion of exploitation. It must be organized to bring out the strengths of the individual, to accommodate his energies, his ideas, talents, and entrepreneurship. Political systems must never suppress or frustrate the creativity or goals of the people they would control.

With the exception of natural ecological systems, all systems are man-made, and therefore subject to abuse. Regardless of whether such control is ultimately for the general good, we are each programmed to place self before societal systems, and egoism marches to its own drum in a pervasive cold war that opposes the very community of which it is a part. It is a popular misconception that those who undermine societal systems are the anarchists and habitual law-breakers, but - given risk-free opportunity and the incentive - societal systems are the target of each and every one of us, placing self-interest before the establishment we helped to found.

With world-wide intelligence accepting the reality that ecological systems must be preserved - with individuals supporting and initiating pollution controls - those with vested interests, such as the industrialists, weigh the impact on profits, and disregard the politician's edict with a hint that they might withdraw financial support for the next political campaign. The politicians conveniently turn a blind eye, and massive pollution continues. Tariffs are imposed to maintain national values, but smuggling is rampant. International fishing rights are agreed upon, only to be broken on a daily basis. Foreign markets must be taken over, monopolized, and expanded.

Overcoming opposition and obstacles is the programmed function of the individual, and he is quite willing to join with others to achieve his goals. Geographical borders are established, but armies march to expand their homeland. Political regimes rise, only to be brought down. The natural confinement of man's world must be expanded into the cosmos, and the natural evolutionary laws that limit our life span must be proven wrong in the pursuit of immortality.

In a free-enterprise, democratic country, run by "honest" politicians, systems per se, whether political, monetary, distributional, gambling, health, or whatever, are merely innocuous sets of rules and routines toward required ends. It is the individual's corrupt use and abuse of systems that is subversive to societal goals, and individuals in government corrupt their own societal goals with their own selfish egoistic ambition.

Systems cannot oppose

A system is never corrupt, never abusive, never anything except an intangible idea that may or may not leave loopholes of opportunity for abuse by those who service and by those who are served. To blame systems for the deviation from required results is to tilt at windmills. It removes blame from those who are guilty beneficiaries, and lays red herrings for those who would have things otherwise. But, unless it is our self-rewarding mandate to reveal fraud, we blame systems because it's easier and less traumatic than confronting guilty individuals or parties. The targeting of any particular group within a system, such as a group of doctors in a national health care system, tends to tar individual doctors with the same opportunistic brush, which is gross injustice to the very small percentage who have only recently entered the health care system.

We are all egoistic individuals, and only actively oppose injustice and dishonesty when we are in some way affected, become its direct victims, or given a paid mandate. Until then we prefer to remain uninvolved, take the easy and safer route, turn a blind eye, and look after number one. Only the very naive stick their necks out without hope of self gain. Many vote for political personalities, without knowing their political platforms, or the alternatives involved. This is not a cynical viewpoint; it's just a fact of life.

Motivations

Each one of us is motivated as an "individual" through a perceived personal need to survive, and as a "social being", through a perceived convenience to that end. One of the great fundamental truths about the human mind is that it is essentially the personal computer of the individual it controls, and is programmed to recognize some advantage to "self" before becoming motivated. Small payment gets desultory performance, but in no way motivates, and the altruisms of the present day are isolated forms of self aggrandizement.

Capitalism, the individual's survival tool

The selfishness of individualism is capitalism at its best. Without excessive encumbrance by societal demands, or the wants and needs of the unsuccessful and poor, and without government intervention, capitalism becomes an upward spiral of re-investment for expansion of plant and renewal of equipment in an insatiable surge for wealth creation. In the creation of a bulkhead against the incidence of poverty, the efforts and strength of the individual paradoxically become the strength of the nation, for wealth creation begets employment and more wealth. It is precisely because the aggression of the individual is multiplied by some millions of workers, that capitalism in America is successful. A beehive is a successful community because each bee uses its initiative to find pollen. Its dance to convey the location and quantity probably serves the dual purpose of also gaining recognition as a valued member of the community. Ants perform in the field as individuals, using collective ingenuity and effort only when it becomes necessary.

Capitalism is successful because it evolved as a natural projection of the need to survive. It is an extension of the individual, who, when threatened by starvation in the cave, became as motivated as a flea fallen from its host. If left alone, and threatened by poverty and all it implies, man shows amazing resourcefulness; he makes contacts, seeks advice and knowledgeable allies, invests his time and money, schemes, worries, connives, exploits, and even works to amass personal wealth. Pragmatic capitalism believes that charity begins at home, and takes advantage of real and selfish priorities, giving little thought to the Utopian idea of sharing.

It is the individualistic nature of capitalism that is transforming national economies to world economies. The recently published book called *Agents of Influence* by P. Choate, highlights the individual's sale of influence to Japanese investors by high ranking government officials in the USA. This is seen as a sell out of privileged trust. It cites huge take-over bids in all of the major American cities, and expresses fear of foreign investment becoming a controlling factor in the American economy. Certainly the selling of influence and inside information is a breach of privileged trust, but expansionism is what competition and free enterprise is all about. In the international concept of free world markets, there is a two-way street, with the gradual abolition of tariffs and the seeking of fresh new markets. A true free-trade system must have limitless growth, despite opinion to the contrary that it kills jobs. It does! But this is the tunneled, short-term perspective of the individual, who will sell armaments to war-mongering nations, crop-spray next to a school, or dump toxic waste in a salmon run, all in the pursuit of profit. We must be ever aware that individuals manipulate systems, and we must have built-in checks and balances in our systems to protect society from egoistic opinion and abuse.

The burden of Socialism

Under a true socialistic regime - without imminent threat of starvation, but deprived of personal wealth, without the right to own property, his actions controlled, and incentive smothered - man becomes a lazy spectator, content to ride on the backs of others. And because of the lack of accountability under a socialistic system, he can get away with it. He may go through the motions of co-operation, but because his rewards are small, his energy and creativity is dissipated in the more rewarding pursuit of a black market. The government pays him a pittance, and he does a commensurate amount of work.

The world learned a profound lesson from Russia's seventy-year experiment with communism - an interchangeable word for radical socialism. It learned what socialism really is, and how it dissipates and suppresses individual effort instead of harnessing it for the betterment of all. Socialism is an idealist's pipe dream, a damaging misconception that misconstrues shared poverty as shared security. It is a panacean fantasy, imposed on the masses by an elite minority that arbitrarily decides that frugality and self-deprivation is good for everyone except those in government, who become a pluralized, privileged, elite power structure.

The saying that "those who are not socialists by the age of twenty are without heart, but those who are not capitalists by the time they're forty are without brains" is probably very near the truth, for pure socialism is the dream of the naive. In the present world it is not even a realistic goal.

If capitalism is an upward spiral, socialism is a downward spiral, taxing and distributing the profits of the successful to subsidize the unsuccessful by diverting funds into depressed areas - either as investments in an attempt to gain a successful momentum, or to alleviate the political discontent in the poorer regions. The result is bitter resentment, the stripping away of further individual incentive, and an eventual general impoverishment.

Socialists are prone to criticize capitalism as being responsible for creating a "dog eat dog world", an exploitation of your fellow man. They charge that the "profit motive" is the rich living off the backs of the poor, but socialism is much more damaging. It is the vast majority of poor living off the backs of the relatively few rich - until there aren't any rich, but only shared poverty. And socialists neglect to consider that any business in the competitive capitalistic world of free enterprise must give satisfaction in order to stay in business, and that any transaction is a two-way agreement, with both parties either believing they are getting the better of the deal, or at least one satisfying a need. Most retail businesses are so anxious to have repeat business that they will gladly exchange goods, or refund money if the customer is dissatisfied. The capitalist makes jobs - even if he sometimes exploits - but unlike the work place under the heavy hand of socialism, no worker is made to stay in a job he doesn't like. He is free to move on and better himself.

The family unit

From the earliest need to co-operate in the hunt and survive, the family unit has resisted individualism and evolved into an innocuous training pod. When free from precocious or misdirected individualism, family units are beautifully balanced generation-relay systems from which powerful dynasties can evolve. We might argue that the co-operation that goes into building dynasties is built on a foundation of either the predictability of greed, the promise of power, or the fear of failure, but the mutual effort still requires a meeting of the minds that transcends generation gaps in a common sustainable goal.

Parents give a child a sense of security and permanence in the here and now. Grandparents on both sides provide a sense of time and perspective, of the past and of the future. It is never a parent's right to deprive a child of this rich heritage by monopolizing his love and restricting his teaching. This is not love. It's possession. It's confinement. It satisfies a need in the mother while stunting the growth of the child.

Adults have no established rights in divorce suits for the struggle to have custody and guardianship. Only children should have rights. The ideal right, barring the tragedy of death or institutionalization, is to be given the security of growing up in a close-knit family, with supportive grandparents, all participating in a broad diversified base of programmed experience. The broader the base, the better able is the child to pick his way through the rubble of inadvertent programmed opinions.

Brothers to brothers provide both physical and mental competitiveness in preparation for the rigors of adulthood, as do sisters to sisters. Sisters to brothers bring out the protective instinct of the latter, and younger brothers to sisters bring out the necessary mothering instinct. Paradoxically, marriage is itself a selfish act by both parties. The success or failure of a marriage can be measured in direct relation to reciprocal needs. As one father advised his son, "If you don't have a need to get married - don't!"

But if capitalism is the natural foraging ground for the individual, then the family unit is his natural working and training base. Because of the increasing societal pressure on the egoistic individual, the family dynasty is now practically extinct. Family break-ups, and the need to be mobile for economic reasons, have fractured many family units - husband from wife, parents from children, and grandparents from grandchildren, and this is a loss to our accumulative, but often opinionated system of programming.

There are two common fallacies within our society. We equate conventional wisdom with that mind-stuffing exercise we call education, and we believe that any formal education is better than any randomly acquired knowledge. The wisdom of the geriatric is judgement with perspective, and is usually learned by the mistakes in the living of life. It is unfortunate that the individualistic lifestyle of the Western world has segregated the young and the aged, for the ones who could most benefit from association with the retiring generation are, - because of their preoccupation with a "higher formal education" - the ones least able to take advantage of the informal association with the elderly. It is for this reason that many university students graduate with a naive knowledge of the real world, and an immature and presumptuous opinion that they are better equipped than the "lesser educated", whereas in truth, their academic knowledge has usually been acquired at the expense of a ponderous five year educational loan, a loss of five years vital experience in the streets of life, and five years loss of income.

They should try sounding out the elderly sometime. They might make up for lost time.

The political spectrum

All political systems in all countries in the world lie along the spectrum between selfish individualism (capitalism) and unselfish (but unrealistic) socialism. Many political parties choose to confuse the issue of their position on the spectrum by adopting obscure names. Capitalism, or selfish individualism, is at the far right of the spectrum, while socialism, or communism, is at the opposite far left. It would be fair to say that left of center of the spectrum lie degrees of socialism with increasing government control, and right of center lies capitalism, with decreasing degrees of government control.

For instance, the social welfare state is not as far left as socialism proper, because unlike socialism that owns everything, the welfare state is content to control everything rather than own it. Sweden is an example of a welfare state, and is currently the highest taxed country in the world: It has to be, in order to have a large enough bureaucracy to enforce and manage the control.

Also to left of center, with varying degrees of government intervention, we have the Labour Party, (as in Britain) and the New Democratic Party, (as in Canada). To the capitalistic immediate right of center, with lessening degrees of government intervention, we have the Democratic Party, (or Liberals) as in the USA, and to the far capitalistic right we have the Republicans, (or Conservatives.) If we move beyond this loose right form of supposedly minimal organized government, we move into anarchy, a state of no government. And periodically, when everyone gets fed up with corrupt politicians, a pragmatic Reform Party comes along choosing to take up any opportunistic position on the entire spectrum.

The one big difference between the capitalists of the USA and those of other countries, is that in England, Canada, and all other capitalistic countries, good government voluntarily refrains from intervention, and allows the people to conduct their lawful business. But the operative word here is "voluntarily", with the government having the right to interfere and legislate social programs at its discretion, which in reality is reserving the right to curtail freedom. In the USA, there is little possibility of unwarranted interference in property ownership, providing taxes are paid and the enterprise lawful. The people control the power of government by legislated checks and balances. It is the difference between "government by the people for the people" or "from the bottom up" government, and from the "top down" authoritarian government. It is the difference of the masses controlling the egoism of the individual, and the individual egoist riding roughshod over the masses.

The political pendulum

It is precisely because we are all individualistically programmed to promote profit to "self", that built-in checks and balances become necessary, for power corrupts. The American Constitution demonstrates an understanding of the tyranny of the individual, and it is so airtight that it would take a revolution to place a socialistic government in power, for the Right Wing Republicans can be sure that the pendulum never swings further toward the center than the Democratic Party. (i.e., a two-party system, both with greater and lesser conservative leanings.) In other countries, all it has taken to nationalize industries, and disallow private ownership of land, has been political promises to a gullible electorate, or the swinging by a majority vote to socialism in a national election - usually as a last ditch attempt to oust an unpopular and blundering Conservative leader. It has taken some thirty-odd years, an iron lady, and a political revolution, for Britain to get back on track after a Labor Government sent the country plummeting into stagnation. It is these fluctuating political swings from right to radical left that keep a country in an unstable poverty, without direction. This is probably why socialists hide their intent by adopting such ambiguous titles as the "New Democratic Party", which is easily confused with the quite different "American Democratic Party".

Even though the flow of power seems to be centralizing around the President of the USA, with the power of veto by congress, their political system is the envy of most of the world. But those countries wishing to emulate its success will need more than just free elections; they will need unalterable legislation that guarantees the continued freedom of the individual. It takes an acclimatized and independent populace that is not forever agitating for hand-outs. The early pioneers of America did more than just tame a wilderness; they programmed those who came after to small expectation and a sense of independence - a quality that is somewhat disappearing with the good life it helped to produce.

The socialist's bait

There are many well-intentioned Americans who believe that there should be a socialized health care system in America. A health care system is the opening gambit of the socialist. It is easily the most justifiable of all social programs, but it is also the insidious thin edge of the wedge, irreversible, and probably the only system that grows tentacles of sub-industries, creating an economy and life of its own, too powerful to be controlled. It is a system (or program) unlike other social systems that are confined in scope to political minorities - the unemployed, the welfare recipients, or the aged, etc. A health care system covers every man, woman, and child, whether healthy or sick! It is a system that caters to the human condition of weakness, and as such gains momentum and popular support as a purportedly free system, until the people become both its addicted victims, and its abusers.

Socialized health care in Canada is now a headless monster that ravages the public purse to promote its own internal economy, until "health" becomes unaffordable because of the redundancy it would bring. In short, it becomes too hot a political potato to be curtailed by any elected government wishing to stay in power. And - without accountability and strong leadership - health care becomes an open barrel for the picking.

Funding of socialized medicine originates and emanates from a centralized branch of government and - without on-the-spot accountability - the system duplicates costly facilities in one town or municipality while depriving another of such facilities. The competition for the tax dollar proliferates grandiose hospital buildings, while placing multi-million-dollar state of the art technology in only a few of the politically high-profile hospitals. It erroneously creates an ill-founded confidence in the people that they are protected by a competent medical profession, with appropriate expertise in all its attending medical paraphernalia. It spawns supporting industries in medical supply conglomerates and drug manufacturing empires, keeps prodigious labor forces employed to service the system - ever more costly with militant unions - and provides “easy access” for exploitation by every hypochondriac within traveling distance by road, rail and air. It raises false expectation and personal disregard for cost, with reassurance founded on the massive budgets extracted from ill-informed and unaware tax payers.

Many who have experienced a socialized health care system - directly or indirectly - have a horror story to tell that is at odds with its pretension and over-use. Those in the system who are unaware of the health care system’s dubious worth, are grateful to have a health net beneath them, something that will prevent worry and bankruptcy. But it is a well known anomaly that one is never at greater risk than when in need of that net, for while pretentious buildings are impressive, they do not a hospital make! A few of the essential ingredients that are missing in most Canadian Provinces aspiring to social health care are: 1. Universal distribution of state of the art equipment, and the expertise to use it. 2. A medical association that demands accountability, professional behavior, and performance, rather than displaying the union syndrome of blind loyalty to its wayward "professional" members. 3. Hospital staffs that are supportive of administrations that seek to beat the yearly budget, rather than prove that the current years funding was insufficient. But we may ask ourselves what is the alternative in a country that provides no alternative to a system touted by its operators (with vested interests) as the best in the world, and a government that is irrevocably and politically "locked in" by an ignorant, dependent, but enthusiastic electorate that thinks health care their God-given right. A government that knows what it can afford, but wants to be re-elected, has only the option to weasel out by inches of attrition. Survivors are terrific advocates, while non-survivors never complain! It is precisely because of the lack of accountability to the taxpayer that no one blows the whistle, and "free" health care remains a top priority.

Christianity, an economic ally

Though the American health care system is not without its faults, and is a non-system that would benefit from radical alteration, its monetary system has an advantage over an Eastern or Middle East country, for in being a Christian country, it has far less restrictive or censorious views on the accumulation of wealth. Christianity not only condones the filthy lucre, but helps support the whole economy - and hence the taxation dollar - by providing a yearly binge in a reciprocal fervor that further impregnates its society with religious piety. Every year the ingenuity of commerce adds to the mass hysteria of Christmas with new and innovative ways of extracting the dollar, with new songs, cards, gifts, films, Broadway shows, feasting and drinking, with nuts, and fruits, and decorating with lights, trees, mistletoe, poinsettias, and holly. Anything goes in the making of merriment and ritual, both indoor and out. The Western economy needs the yearly impetus of the Christmas trade, but again, a yearly celebration could just as well be based on love and life, rather than the theoretical birth date of a one time cult leader.

Conversely, in other Eastern countries where religion and a subsistent level of living are considered the gateway to paradise, the people are inured to hardship and have little incentive to improve standards. Few have experienced wealth and abundance, and most abject poverty.

In recent years, satellite TV has seduced the Third World to seek revenge, if not retribution. The people of the sand and of the naked African plains have been permitted to look into the drawing rooms of the Western world and contrast an easy life style with their own shabby and grueling existence. The result has been resentment and bitter confusion, with those especially devout becoming motivated to violent reaction. For the virus of discontent is at odds with a religious conviction that discounts worldly possessions, making it easier to die for a cause that has shaped their sacrificial lives. In a third world that is militarily weak, terrorism is the answer to what they consider injustice.

Although most Middle East countries are really wealthy, their money either stagnates in pools of wealth, or is invested abroad. And that is what it is all about. That is our difference and our warring reason. The Western mentality of those walking, talking, biological computers who follow the Christian faith, are uninhibited by the accumulation of wealth and are individually programmed to pursue economic fulfillment. They are able to plug into a compatible network of like-thinkers desirous of keeping the money moving. For it is not the amount of money that makes a country wealthy so much as the velocity of its movement in the upward spiral. A central planning agency under a socialistic regime could never duplicate the complexity and volume of interrelated thought that is stimulated by a free-from-government-intervention nation in a free-wheeling market place.

Insidious effects of prolonged Socialism on Individualism

Prolonged socialism inures the individual to deprivation by degree, and deprives him of initiative. But in the long term it does more than that; it takes away individualism and replaces it with dependency - one of the most devastating losses experienced by the aged - a sense of achievement through “self”. Individuality and sexuality are the two redeeming humanistic qualities that save us from being robotic automatons.

The Russian people have lost more than their sense of humor - a psychological weapon to combat hardship - they also lost a flock of golden geese when their satellite countries gained independence, and such a loss will take more than one generation to recover. The people of the now defunct Soviet Union have been nursed too long in the cradle of a corrupt government. Hardship challenges individuality and is the natural condition to motivate; the individual continues to respond even after receiving the reward of small successes.

The greatest challenge that faced Gorbachev was not the dismantling of communism, but the rehabilitation of the Russian people back to selfish and independent individualism, (or capitalism) with its motivating drive and initiative that would revitalize the economy. The rehabilitation of Russia has been such a dismal failure that now the older people who enjoyed the state cradle want to revert back to communism, saying they had more pride and never had to beg for food under the old regime.

This is true. After the second world war Moscow impoverished its satellite countries - Poland, Yugoslavia, Czechoslovakia, Hungary, the Baltic States etc - by skimming off the cream of their production, loading it up on specially scheduled trains, and wholesaling it in the Russian zone. In truth, they created a system of satellite slavery. This General Aleksandr Lebed of the new order who seeks to overthrow Yelsin and reinstate communism, has small opportunity to repeat the exploitation that topped up the Russian bread-basket and fed its populace, since all hell would break loose if he ever tried to repeat such a system. The deprivation of East Germany has been of a shorter duration, and having closer ties with the affluent West Germans, there is a perceived incentive that could bring about a quicker absorption into a culture of higher expectation. However, even these two "brothers at arms" are experiencing some difficulty in their comparative attitudes.

We fortunates who have been raised and programmed under a capitalistic regime have developed something of the "Artful Dodger" philosophy, a sort of wheeling-dealing independence that can take its lumps, and recognize a vacuum cleaner salesman from a Jehovah's witness through a slat in the blind at a distance of fifty paces. It is a skill, or rather an attitude, not easily acquired.

But socialism does not necessarily come about by revolution or election; it can also evolve as the result of a slow and insidious deterioration, with either the introduction of popular sounding social programs by governments traveling under false colors, or grandiose national programs that inhibit the re-investment necessary to maintain the economic upward spiral. World history is strewn with the remains of broken empires brought about by egoistic individuals over-extending their drive for control: Britain, Portugal, Spain, France, China, Russia - to name a few defunct empires. The USA is presently in imminent danger of breaking its upward economic spiral by inhibiting reinvestment through misdirection of funds into grandiose programs for Space travel, Star Wars, Stealth Bombers, and by aspirating to be the world's watch dog for democracy and freedom. Expansion depends on re-investment. It is the difference between giving the economy a transfusion, and bleeding it, which is what socialism does in its attempts to redistribute wealth.

Socialism by default.

In capitalistic jurisdictions such as England and Canada, it is the licence to give promiscuous option to the whole spectrum of political choice by free election that can result in the erosion of the freedom of the individual. Socialism gets into office through unenlightened choice, and creates precedents in the form of "freebie" programs with which other so-called Liberals and Conservatives compete for votes while inadvertently socializing their countries by degrees. During Pierre Trudeau's term of office as a "Liberal" prime minister, Canada became more culturally divided, more socialistic, and had more social programs than any other capitalist country. He made the mistake of calling out the National Guard to quell the unrest of his own people of Quebec!

If anyone is more responsible for the drive for the separation of Quebec from the rest of Canada, it was General de Gaulle, who, when on a visit to Quebec, shouted the rallying cry of the French, "Viva la Quebec." Since that time Quebecers have viewed themselves as being in bondage rather than congratulating themselves on being the most privileged Province of Canada. Quebec has traditionally had more Prime Ministers than any other Province, received more Federal funding, been granted more plums in the form of government contracts, and experienced more tourism and export trade than any other Province of Canada. The rest of Canada has in fact been making concessions to Quebec from day one. Their grievance has been nurtured on the difference in language alone, rather than on economic deprivation.

And Brian Mulroney, of the Canadian "Progressive" Conservatives, inadvertently followed suit by treading the path of appeasement, and buying more votes with more innocuous sounding social programs that would have had to be paid for with heavier taxation. His proposed child day-care program, set aside through lack of money and a preoccupation for fame on the world scene, is a page out of the socialist's book. However, with a more enlightened population, politicians are finding it increasingly difficult to buy popularity and leadership with taxpayers" money.

There is in effect a general blending of socialism and capitalism in both the Eastern and Western countries that weakens the West with socialism and strengthens the East with capitalism. It is the accumulation of social programs that brings a country down, because as they accumulate they increase expectation, and once a perceived "freebie" is introduced, it is political suicide for subsequent governments to discontinue them for any reason what-so-ever.

It is an accepted fact that the bureaucracy of a socialistic state is of necessity many times larger than that required for a capitalistic state, and the bureaucracy increases in direct proportion to the number of socialistic programs. It is interesting to note that while Canada's population has increased only threefold since 1930, its bureaucracy has increased thirteen fold, and income tax has gone from zero to more than sixty-four percent.

With the imposition of the GST (Goods and Services Tax), on January 1991, tax freedom day moved from July to August of a working year. That is to say that a Canadian working man will be required to work eight months of a year just to pay his taxes. And taxes will continue to increase until the profit motive has been purged from the system and capitalism degenerates to socialism with a continuing spiral of taxes. It is such greed that ensures continuing inflation. Canadians are the victims of an elitist establishment that seeks to enhance its own power by beating its own system. But paradoxically, it is the average man in the street who imagines he's beating the system by agitating for more "free" socialized programs.

The Canadian Liberals and the so-called Progressive Conservatives have emulated socialist governments in the political shell game. Like all governments, they have no independent financial means to throw behind their programs other than their legislated right to tax the populace. Federal governments preach frugality by depriving the Provincial governments of their share structure of taxes, while at the same time elevating their own power structure and personal life styles.

The only difference between a dictatorship and socialism is that one is singular with unilateral access to tyranny, while the other is plural and requires a consensus. Pluralism gives socialism a more palatable degree of legitimacy. i.e., Control under a socialist government emanates from a full blown committee, and is masked by propaganda and the distribution of "freebies". The only ones who really collect are the capitalistic-socialists who run the system.

Self interest - or need - is the motivational driving force behind all human endeavor. Those programmed to look for leadership will join any political group or cult in the search for direction, whether it be a neo-Nazi organization, flower cult, or the church. Only early programming or opportunity will decide where they'll go. A politician will join the dog-catcher's association to get elected, or will compromise his platform to include religious dogma in exchange for a 45% voting body.

Newt Gingrich's contract is not with America. It's with James Dobson, a conservative surfing the hundred million dollar television airways under the banner of Evangelism. Gingrich's contract came into effect when he became a Republican candidate. It was implied that he would serve the American people in the capacity expected of him, and he just breached that contract by polarizing American politics, and equating his political platform with Christianity. Beware the political/religious alliance for it seeks only mind control and the vote.

Whether for material or intangible benefit, whether it be positive wealth, power, or high profile image, or the negative threatened loss of esteem, loss of support, or love - the incentive to go into politics, go to church, rob a bank or write a book, is self-interest or need, if only in a masochistic form.

—There is a universal myth that self-determination is an ever-present option, but only a strong self-image based on viable truth can make self-determination a reality.

CHAPTER 12

Power and opportunity

Manufacturers of large and small companies have learned the lesson that they must listen to, and heed, the messages of need conveyed by public demand. Failure to do so almost certainly results in the demise of their companies, for both the knowledge of the changing needs of succeeding generations, and the technology that satisfies those needs, are the vital ingredients that can create power and opportunity.

Technological information and monopolistic production are the prime objectives for some twenty-five countries competing in the headlong race for economic world supremacy. However, information for a country is not synonymous with information for individual companies. Information for a country is both power and opportunity, because countries have the resources to make their own opportunity. Information for the would-be entrepreneurs is potential power, but does not necessarily include the opportunity to use it to make things happen.

For countries jockeying for position in the economic race that holds the possibility of wealth or war, information is the most sought after starting point. Countries, whether friendly or hostile, resort to military, industrial and commercial espionage. They have organized espionage offices and spy teams operating out of practically every city in the world. Such information is the power that drives human endeavor, and determines the future of their companies. They guard their information like gold bullion in a vault.

However, not all production is geared to the wishes of the people. Visionaries, politicians, appointed agents, and scientists are the privileged few who have the power and opportunity to speak for, and commit society to costly expenditures. The masses have no need, and perhaps no desire, to travel to other planets, but visionaries see a benefit to future generations, and through the politicians, secure the funding to support their visions. Politicians in government decide to spend billions on armaments, war planes, tanks, or submarines, that they think essential for the security of the country, and, after voting these potentates into power, the people have no alternative but to pay the required taxes in order to follow their directives.

President Bush, in his State of the Union address, January 29th 1991, spoke of giving more power and opportunity to the individual. President Bush placed so much emphasis on the idea that he repeated the theme no less than four times, and we might infer from his remarks that he meant legalized opportunity, not illicit opportunity to ravage and beat social systems. His speech implied the taking away of political restrictions that are inhibiting the programmed individual from doing what he does best if given the chance. i.e: Accumulate wealth like a squirrel collecting nuts in the fall. The taking away of restrictions, such as high taxation, and the making available of low interest loans, would be providing the opportunity that spurs incentive.

However, the concept of "giving more power and opportunity to the people" is the promise of a politician carried away with his own rhetoric. One can designate responsibility. One can provide opportunity. One can bestow rank, and rank implies power, but rank is not power. One cannot bestow power on the people. Power per se is not power unless it is wanted and used. A milk-sop king, who has inherited his rank, has the potential for power, but a show of power never materializes. One must want power, seize it, and wield it. While true information might lead to power, power is not dependent on true information. Power is a nebulous or multi-faceted attribute; among others, there is political power, financial power, charismatic power, the power of knowledge, the power to do good, the power to bring down, and - the most powerful power of all - the power to designate responsibility, demand accountability, and effect meaningful change from a position of power. We tend to confuse and interchange responsibility, which is a designated obligation, with power, which is an intangible and unilateral possession of control. Power can of course imply responsibility, but power is not responsibility.

President Bush was talking about freeing the initiative of the frustrated unemployed, for that is where the dormant strength of any country lays. He was not talking about the pie-in-the-sky problems of future generations. He was talking about the here and now. He was talking about accommodating the programmed individual within the framework of an environment of need. In other words, training him and having him gainfully employed.

In the complicated world of today, training or programming has never been such an important requirement. The idea of training for specific positions is not new of course. Even at the time when our American ancestors were early pioneers, independent, innovative individuals who rebelled against the misused power that created tyranny in the old world, they endeavored to train for specific occupations.

The pioneers that came to America to carve out a niche for themselves in the wilderness of a free and unoppressed land - it was in truth, an uncontrolled, system-free land - were successful beyond their wildest dreams. For scrambling for a living by competing with animals in the wilderness was man's legacy and forte. At that time a strong arm and a dauntless spirit were the essential attributes for full employment. Such aggressive and unafraid heroes were legion. Their sense of fairness and co-operation - founded on virgin opportunity and the need to survive - created a fortuitous democracy that inculcated the basic principles of freedom written down by the Fathers of Confederation, and embraced by succeeding generations.

When taken out of context, opportunity is also a nebulous or ambiguous concept. Opportunity for what? Without explanation, we can only conclude that the promise of more power and opportunity for the individual is an optimistic but ambiguous promise. Unfortunately, the American people never had the opportunity to find out what the President meant, as his own political opportunity was not forthcoming.

If we could again find an environment that in itself would reward full-time endeavor, there would be no more unemployment. However, in the reality of the present day, there is of course only one way to endow an individual with productive power, and that is by investing it in his person; to educate, and specifically program him to self-rewarding endeavor. But without the further opportunity to put the teaching into practice, he is still without a job. You can teach a man to put a new roof on a house, but without giving him the tools, shakes, and a ladder to get up there, he's still unproductive and without income.

If we want to solve the unemployment problem, it's not enough to educate, or program to self-rewarding endeavor. It is not enough to make a judgement of society's perceived need at any given time and direct mass programming toward that end. About the time when Henry Ford's first Model T came rolling off the assembly line, everyone was going to be a motor mechanic. The result was a superfluity of unemployed mechanics. When television became a reality, everyone thought that television repair was the coming need, and we ended up with so many unemployed television repair men, that most had to rethink their careers. The same thing happened with computers, and now we would have more computer-oriented unemployed than there are in the actual work force if it were not for the fact that computers have been an ongoing development of improvements in a growing technology. Furthermore, computerized knowledge lends itself to a very large variety of businesses.

We must program in accordance with the individual and diversified interests of the unemployed. They may take longer to become absorbed into the work force, but we will end up with a long term, more efficient, more contented working population. We must also supply the opportunity for the unemployed to use their new information. We must give them the tools, make available low interest bank loans to those entrepreneurs with ambition, and a good story to tell. We must provide opportunity for them to go into business for themselves, without being taxed out of existence, or at a level that would inhibit re-investment in necessary expansion. In the recent past we've loaned and given billions of dollars to developing countries. We accept the fact that billions will have to be written off as uncollectible, but we baulk at petty loans on the home front. Loans that will give the economy a kick start. There will of course be bad debts, but this can be minimized with proper screening procedures.

In Canada, there is the Federal Business Development Bank, with the case counselors largely staffed by knowledgeable retired business executives. It would be a productive innovation to have government teams of paid consultants spend a couple of weeks with new businesses, to overlook and advise on progressive business practices. Their expenses could be reimbursed when the successful operation becomes productive.

When President Bush spoke of giving more power and opportunity to the individual, he was probably advocating intensifying capitalism on a broader base. He was advocating that we do things the American way, and not leave the individual to scavenge among social systems. Small businesses have long been recognized as the basis of a growing, pervasive opportunity that contributes to society by providing opportunity for others. It is a capitalistic, self-building system, far removed from the socialistic philosophy of sharing the wealth by providing "freebies" at the expense of the successful, or opportunities to rip off tax systems and deplete the public purse.

To give more power and opportunity to the individual, would mean less power for local government, and in turn less power for state and the centralized Federal Government, for - regardless of the fact that power is non-transferable - one cannot relinquish responsibility and still retain it. Alvin Toffler speaks of decentralization in his book, *The Third Wave,* and this in effect is suggesting the delegating of fiscal responsibility to the grass root level, where localized needs are better understood and earmarked. Remote control and spending by centralized government is both uninformed and wasteful, but rarely do we find an enlightened politician who is willing to relinquish any sphere of responsibility in order for the country to become more efficient in its use of resources, and perhaps in the doing pay off its national debt. On the other hand local politicians, when given the opportunity, are - by and large - as prone to playing self-rewarding games as are federal politicians.

CHAPTER 13

The Information Age

They call this the "Information Age" because over the last thirty years computers and communication technology have come together, to bring the power of detailed information into every facet of our lives. It's been proven that with the right information we can reach the moon, and this information has brought the stars a little closer. With the right information we've prolonged life, and this makes immortality also seem a little closer. Anything and everything is becoming a conscious challenge, and every challenge brings forth specialists to supply related information that shrinks the problem, equating reality with aspects of science fiction.

Information runs our private lives. Statistical and market information runs big business; the money market, the bond market, treasury bills, strip coupons, stocks and shares. Information controls land use, lumber, fishing and other industries. Statistical information supplies us with our population census, record of political constituencies, and the manipulation of people that goes into its making. Relevant information motivates and empowers. Information points direction. Without it we're lost in a purposeless void.

The "information age" has quickened communication. It has helped human memory. It has combined technologies to provide us with easy transference of, and access to, prodigious data banks. But technology has done nothing for the content or the integrity of the information it carries, and without this fundamental form of quality control, we are still living in the misinformation age, for the unbridled imaginings of the human mind are still the originators of erroneous and primitive concepts that we enshrine in our electronic archives.

By non-denial and omission, we endorse all information, false or true, and send it scooting down the information highway to create traffic jams of ambiguity for those struggling to deal in truth. Scientists waste precious time in their short lives feeling obligated to debate obsolete and unscientific theories on creationism. School Boards agonize on appropriate curricula, and teachers flee in frustration because those in authority are unable to relinquish their early programming. For the sake of posterity and sanity, and to obviate the risk of society being led up blind alleys, there must be an authorized licencing authority to authenticate the degree of truth in information, especially the kind of manipulative political propaganda being fed the populace. The news media should have filled this role by investigation and authentication of truth in unbiased, non-political reporting, but instead publishers have opted for sensationalism to achieve greater sales volume. If it was possible to emulate the tabloids and print fiction while retaining a germ of truth, there'd be eighty-pound babies proliferating the globe, and B47s on the moon. Unfortunately, we must look to more responsible and less profit-motivated institutions to investigate the truth and keep the people informed.

With the coming of communication technology that can reach the world through instantaneous satellite broadcast, we have the most manipulative controlling device ever placed at a government's disposal. There has never been a greater need for an independent authority, affiliated with schools and universities with research departments throughout the land, to become the arbiters of truth versus opinion. This is not being subversive of democratic governmental control. It's merely keeping it directed on line. After all, democracy means the appraisal and involvement of the people, and governments can be wrong as demonstrated by the Vietnam war. The insidious spread of opinion as fact - government propaganda, medical, and church dogma, antiquated beliefs, lies, and biased distortions of special interest groups - should be examined before being promulgated as causation for support or confrontation.

The Information Age coincides with the build-up of the world's largest nuclear arsenals. There are currently large quantities of uranium, used in the making of the nuclear bomb, being smuggled into Germany. The authorities believe the theft and smuggling are coming out of Russia, which supposedly has its supplies under top security. It could mean that the skin heads of Germany have somehow obtained financial backing, and are again looking for confrontation on a revised scale, or that Iraq is again girding its loins for war. It could also mean that terrorists are again planning their worst on the world scene. Whatever it means, we can no longer afford to squabble over fictitious issues or be led into war by people with vested interests and a sense of righteous indignation.

The bomb is a fact of life. A scientific truth, if you will. Its proliferation already a fait accompli. Its eventual use is a foregone conclusion and only a matter of time. We cannot ban the bomb. We cannot defuse it universally, and we cannot, in the given time frame, find, define, and re-program the hate that will inspire its use. We can only defuse the emotional and misleading rhetoric that can lead to the mass killings. We can only use truth to defuse the aberrational behavior that will be the result of perhaps inadvertent but provocative challenge. It must be the responsibility of every national agency to recognize and expose the half-truths that inflame and evoke response. We must not placate those who are viciously programmed, but neither must we support one-sided argument and opinion by accepting "news" at its face value, or by reiterating government-approved history and propaganda, sometimes ignoring (or ignorant of) the political or economic ramifications behind our nationalistic stance.

The simple idea of teaching the concept that substantiated truth must be separated from beliefs and opinions as a qualification for all subjects taught in schools, is never considered. Indeed, many of our teachers actively teach falsehoods as truths without fear of censure, with the result that most of our young people actually believe that Columbus "discovered" America, and that before this fortuitous happening, America had been an isolated chunk of land, inhabited by lost savages of little consequence. Many believe that in the Gulf war, America became involved for the sole purpose of rescuing the poor people of Kuwait. They are never taught that this reason was incidental to the threat of America having to pay higher prices for oil sold through a more monopolistic Iraq. They're not informed that the President of the USA had substantial oil holdings and a personal stake in the issue. As said before, many young people still doubt that the Jewish holocaust ever happened, or that, contrary to the creationist's teachings within religious schools, evolution is now an established scientific fact. None of us know whether government keeps the recorded facts of flying saucers under wraps, or whether we are surrounded by hallucinating kooks. Would the Warren Commission, appointed in November of 1963 to pontificate on the Kennedy assassination, have so blatantly fudged the evidence to support their contention that there was a single assassin, if an independent investigative agency had been in force at the time? Would the world still be guessing at the truth?

In her book, *The Cure For All Cancers*, Hulda Regehr Clark, PH.D., ND, stated categorically that all cancers are caused by a particular parasite that can be killed in five days, and kept from re-occurring with a maintenance prescription together with the discarding of all carcinogenic household products. Is this researcher right? Has this one person succeeded when a world-wide multi-billion dollar cancer-cure industry has failed - after some eighty years of research? The cancer-cure industry is thriving on fear, and is getting a reputation for its prodigious size and its failure to find a solution. The very least it could do would be to either publicly repudiate or support this researcher's findings.

Hulda Clark is obviously an extremely intelligent and credible researcher. She goes on to say that whereas this parasite, when found as an adult in the liver - in the presence of propyl alcohol - causes cancer, it also causes diabetes when found in the pancreas in the presence of wood alcohol. If found in the thymus - together with benzene - it causes HIV disease, and in the brain, with either toluene or xylene, it causes Alzheimer's disease. In the kidneys, in the presence of solvents, it causes either Hodgkin's disease, endometriosis of the uterus or chronic prostatitis of the prostate. And when in the skin, it causes Kaposi's sarcoma. Are these facts right? If they are, surely Clark should at the very least be receiving the Pulitzer Prize for research. But where is the medical establishment on this? People need answers. They need confirmation or denial from the accepted authorities, and they need an established truth agency to see that they get it.

We don't know whether religious scholars, muffled by programmed bias, or agonizing over an economic conflict of interest, are sitting on disclosures from the Deep Sea Scrolls. There are no impartial overseers to eliminate their bias. The available material was distributed among a limited number of religious scholars for their interpretation, and tunnel vision could prompt them to misinterpret and authenticate their established beliefs. The portions that have been released has been highly contradictory to the established dogma of the church, and many "scholars" would consider it a breach of trust to disillusion the devotees of Christianity with conflicting or denigrating interpretations. We don't even know whether vital pieces of the disclosure have been destroyed. The list of arbitrary issues and questionable happenings go on and on.

The screening for truth must start with education. Schools and Universities should be closely allied with branches of Central Intelligence Agencies that are disassociated from their governments in an expanded mission to fill this essential role. They should be upgraded in expertise, purpose, and function, with computerized input into information banks, utilizing Internet and other world-wide information sources as confirmatory agencies, in addition to the established world news media, and other special research facilities for assessing the degree of truth on both sides of any confrontational issue. All such independent agencies should be tested for neutral and non-political bias, just like the judiciary tests for impartiality with juries, and all should maintain close liaison with the news media, in order to perform an essential function as the disseminators of different viewpoints and established truths - a function that is fifty years overdue. Governments have to make unilateral decisions to declare war behind closed doors. War is not an issue for a referendum, but neither should it be a precipitous venture without comprehensive debate by informed parties. Society must not tolerate a penalty for blowing the whistle on phony information. The excuse that public disclosure might damage national security is no longer valid in a world of nuclear threat that can come from either side of a confrontation.

The sheer volume of arbiters to any confrontation would impose diplomatic discussion rather than precipitous violence. This is not idealism. This is precaution in a world that lives on a knife's edge. One can imagine Hitler's change of tactics in the initial stages of his war-mongering moves for world dominance, if he had been subjected to the immediacy of the discerning eye of the world. His whole dictatorship technique was to advance piece-meal over the smaller countries until the German nation had the confidence that he was an unstoppable, invincible oracle. It is doubtful whether he would have signed treaties in bad faith, having every intention of breaking them. The same could be said for every dictatorial leader that uses propaganda to further his own selfish ambition.

Investigative institutions should cease to be outreach agencies for government propaganda, or re-enforcing institutions for the church, and concentrate on exposing manipulative opinion for the damaging controlling device that it is. Truth is always verifiable and supportable. When it isn't, it's still opinion. However, because the financing authority usually calls the tune, and demands loyal adherence to its policies, governments should also surrender the purse strings and the fiscal budgeting of the various ministries to separate independent audited bodies, with each ministry being responsible for staying within its allocated budget. By breaking up fiscal responsibility, there would be greater control of the taxpayer's dollar. It's been amply demonstrated that governments throughout the world are incapable of handling money.

Lobbies by the tobacco manufacturing industry, contending that nicotine is not addictive, must be publicly exposed for the damaging sales pitch that it is - no matter who has vested interests in the industry. Doctors who are aware that a diagnosis of HIV positive is not necessarily a death sentence - that AIDS does not necessarily follow - are maintaining the subterfuge as a disincentive to promiscuity. A justifiable ploy, you might think, but the falsehood is causing unnecessary despair, premature deaths and suicides. Even the medical profession must not use manipulative opinion. If there is one requirement of all institutions, whether public service or private enterprise, it is not to suppress or misrepresent the truth. The collective wisdom of the people can cope with the truth, and give their support to the correct decisions of an elite minority.

Not-with-standing the flawed programming of individual teachers, educational institutions have an obligation to differentiate between truth and opinion, and to make students aware that some text books are extremely biased. There is also an obligation to screen the integrity of the educators, and to make students aware that truth shall be the mandate in the curriculum.

Unfortunately, by the time children start kindergarten at the age of five, parental pre-school programming has often biased or seriously impaired the child. Until parents in general realize their own flaws, and voluntarily limit the parameters of their influence, we cannot expect true education of the child while depending on the vagaries of the parents.

The high sounding phrase “religious freedom” is a damaging misnomer for what is really freedom to brain-wash and program young children to any ridiculous belief. It is a dangerous and misleading assumption that the violence of the present day is attributable to the lack of reverence for religious teaching. It is the confusion of conflicting programming that causes aberrational behavior. The freedom of information act is yet another theoretically high-sounding phrase. It is another right that can only be won with a fight. In practice, egoistic leaders tell the people only that which they think will support the correctness of their political stance. Since our early beginnings, opinions have been misrepresented as truth. Succeeding generations have placed their trust and their lives on the knowledge and integrity of parents and teachers who are themselves victims of haphazard programming, and nothing is about to change unless we change it.

For decades we have debated the relative merits of subjects taught in schools, whether they really contribute in a relevant and meaningful way to the task of earning a living. Academics channel those they consider less gifted, less able to handle abstract concepts, into vocational institutes to learn welding, carpentry and plumbing etc. Though it is obvious that not all students are gifted in the same way, we inculcate insecurity by innuendo, and place value only on channeled aptitudes. By implication we deprive students of their sense of confidence. Children of all ages who are weak achievers along the accepted guidelines are aware of having a comparative lack of respect and feel the stress of inadequacy.

Psychiatrists, psychologists, and other "professional experts," have been on an I.Q. kick for the last sixty years. They've categorized children into various levels of inadequacy, and programmed failure in many millions who have been unfortunate enough to score low on their constrictive tests. But these misguided "specialists" who have listened to and believed the opinions of those who would seek to control the direction of human development, have only proven their own limitations as a consequence.

As long as educational systems throughout the world sift their students for those judged "gifted," meaning those pupils who conform to the tunnel-visioned criteria of selected subject and I.Q. testing, they will project negative programming. With limited budgets, limited thinking, and limited criteria, these education systems concentrate on these relatively few conformers, and produce a small percentage of successes, a somewhat larger mediocrity, and a preponderance of failures.

Intelligence cannot be measured by a number called a quotient. The human mind is far more than a Pandora's box that leads children to smoking, drugs, drink and crime. The human mind is full of surprises of positive potential that has diversified untapped creativity and ability.

Intelligence manifests itself in so many different ways; it comes through the hands, through visual perception and interpretation, through inner conceptualization, through spatial awareness, through memory, cross-referencing and the association of ideas, through co-ordination, and appreciation of harmony and sound. We find intelligence in curiosity, perseverance, comparison, judgement, balance, appropriateness, and even survival. The pursuit and recognition of truth and the rejection of incompatible opinion is probably the most important facet of intelligence. Trying to measure intelligence by awarding a number is like measuring the capacity of the ocean in linear feet. And a child's mind is a comparatively blank sheet of paper. He hasn't had time to develop many of these "intelligences" much less accumulate experiences to store in his memory bank.

Contrary to popular belief, emotion itself is a contributing factor to, or a detracting factor of intelligence. The ability to use emotion to inspire effort, to enthuse others to a cause or purchase, or to dissuade them from an action, is pure intelligence. A salesman without enthusiasm makes a poor living. Emotion becomes a negative only when reason loses control to despair or anger, or when it blocks acceptance to a logical revision of an early programming.

In truth, by failing to recognize that every child is unique, with untapped potential - not necessarily falling within the accepted guidelines of the "experts" - many teachers transmit negative opinions that program children into believing that ditch-digging machines have deprived them of their only hope of earning a living. And disappointed parents reenforce this negativism by believing and giving credence to the teacher's opinion, since after all he is a professional in his own right. We neglect to realize that he is also a product of a similarly limited mentor.

Children must be taught that their teachers are not infallible, and that they are no better or worse than themselves in many areas of learning; that some teachers have indeed been misprogrammed by opinion. We are all human with human failings and we need programming that will enhance those areas that have appealed to our interest, but essentially we must be programmed to differentiate between established truth and opinion.

Society has created rarefied authorities with licence to expound opinion without challenge. They're called "professionals," and only the most argumentative and aggressive of non-professionals have the temerity to question their opinion - unless it were to ask for further professional opinion. True, professional opinions are usually conclusions based on programmed assessment of surrounding facts, but the intelligent layman should still question, and realize that these assessments are often biased opinions of arrogant thinkers, neither comprehensive nor conclusive.

—The question "Who's pulling your strings?" can most certainly be answered in the plural. It's everyone, past and present, who has caused a synapse within your mind by passing on an idea that is now a part of you. Ideas can jump generation gaps and flow through societies like a river through a receptive channel. Your strings have been pulled with lasting ideas, some conceived eons before you were born. And you can be sure that each and every string-puller was, in his time, a victim of much string pulling.

CHAPTER 14

To Begin the Weaning

Though capable of intricate and profound thought, man emerged from the dark middle ages with little factual knowledge upon which to hang his hat. Largely because of the church, his range of interest had been confined to speculative philosophy, witch hunts, and tentative and imaginative astrology, all controlled by the dogmatic and authoritarian establishment of the church, and the fear of the unknown. In the choice between good and evil, the perceived alternative to the sin of sex and violence was complete surrender to the church. With the exception of the rare thinker, who was usually a persecuted outcast, there was little challenge to church dogma.

We have reached an evolutionary fork in the last century by way of a rapid accumulation of factual knowledge that has provided us with a true base for reasoning. Though not comprehensive, this new base is beginning to replace the speculative opinions of our early beginnings. However, our progress is still seriously impaired by the ongoing concentration of programming in obsolete beliefs. The entire world is permeated with the fanaticism of religion that starts in the cradle and ends in the grave.

The Western world has cartoons of the complete old and new testaments that program the toddlers who sit on the floor around the television. There are bible comics for those just learning to read. Television programs bombard the would be intellectuals with facts pertaining to the historical accuracy of the bible, insinuating that such proof supports the spirituality of man, and the legitimacy of Jesus as the son of God. We have organized mass hysteria, hate and wars for those already programmed, and priests and politicians who reenforce beliefs by surfing on the emotions of the masses.

Our only hope for mental emancipation for our future generations lies in the parents. They must start protecting their children against the obsolete and harmful influences of society, rather than continuing to perpetuate beliefs as mindless victims. We are rightfully concerned with the prospect of our children inheriting a legacy of national debt, but we should be far more concerned that they may inherit the legacy of the repeating time bomb, the legacy of possible death and destruction that has been carried down over generations, going back so far that it has become accepted as one of the hazards of living. The world our children inherit is doomed to continual conflict, confusion and genocide if we allow them to be molded by the insidious effects of seemingly innocuous programming.

Furthermore, parents must not be naive and think they are raising little emancipated free thinkers merely because they ignore the religious bias that surrounds them. The religious influence of the society in which we live is an insidious and pernicious influence that will invade the stoutest walls, and only complete awareness and understanding of what it will do - how it can and will affect their lives - will render it harmless.

The aberrational behavior that has so little regard for human life is the result of misinformation, misinterpretation, and hate propaganda; messages that distort judgement and incite a hate reaction. We said that to sleep with hate is to be in bed with a viper. Every automaton in the 1945 Nazi Party was consumed with hate, and even at the Nuremberg trials, never realized that his imminent death sentence was the result of his irrevocable programming. However, causation of the holocaust, as chronicled herein, conveys a message that will deeply affect anyone who recognizes and interprets it. Those of a religious persuasion won't like it, for it implies gullibility, and denies the harmlessness of their beliefs.

Those who are confirmed homosexuals won't like the message contained herein either, for it supports the contention that they are the victims of programmed, perverted sexual behavior; an unsavory connotation compared to their being victims of genetic defects. If we look into the brain structure of habitual drug addicts, and child molesters, we would again see what appears to be basic genetic differences from the norm. And the longer the addiction the more pronounced would be these differences. However, because the brain produces a variety of reinforcing chemicals geared to ensure perpetuation of a habitual behavioral pattern, homosexuals could take the optimistic view that, though not likely - or even desired - this disclosure holds the possibility for a cure by enforced prolonged self-change.

Homosexual child molesters won't like the message either, not because they are pleading genetic defects, but because it brings home the truth of their addiction, and their forceful or subtle pursuit of sexual satisfaction at the expense of innocent and defenseless children. Society ostracizes child molesters as one step lower than the rapist, who also displays total disregard for equal participation by consenting and knowledgeable adults. Society's revulsion for the child molester negates any chance for his rehabilitation.

The isolated, sex-driven molesters of goats, pigs, or whatever satisfies their unscratchable itch - which fortunately make up a very small segment of the population - will like the message, for it equates the power of their sex drive with the rest of humanity.

Some geriatrics, depending on their mind frame, won't like the message, for it makes a lifetime of worship an empty void. Even if these oldsters could change their psyche - which they can't - it would afford them little time to be comfortable with such drastic changes in their outlook, beliefs and lifestyles. Indeed, far better they had not read this book! However, it is extremely unlikely that this book will damage the lives of those who rely on their religion to get through the day. Most will not take in more than three chapters, and those who do will continue to believe in their own "truths," simply because they want to, and because it will take more than a book to change their programming. Those who have been irrevocably programmed to a need to believe in a sponsoring god, are far better continuing their established lifestyle, for a lifetime of worship shouldn't end embroiled in controversy and doubt.

Many beleaguered Germans will like the message, providing their religion doesn't get in the way of their exoneration, for it demonstrates that those who have suffered fifty years of scorn and blame for being a member of a particularly cruel race, are in fact - with the single exception of language - no different from the rest of humanity. They nurture hate, listen to, and heed megalomaniacal and fulminating leaders, and thus become vulnerable to manipulation by propaganda. Those programmed Germans (or skinheads wherever they are) who would rather be dictated to than think and assess for themselves, are in fact sociologically immature.

In the following suggested behavioral change we're not looking for rebellion against political, working, or family authority; we're searching for mental emancipation in thought. We're searching for maturity and truth, both in ourselves and in others. When we find it we will understand that, like catching a contagious cold, there is no blame in either the giver or the getter, the programmer or the programmed. However, there is a lack of awareness and vigilance on the part of those who are so easily programmed.

Mental emancipation is achieved within the confines of one's own mind. You don't have to live a life of confrontation with the victims of zealotry or the radical automatons that surround you. You merely let your thoughts, beliefs and conclusions be guided by your own programming in deciding between what is opinion and what is truth. Maintain an amenable and agreeable facade while practicing that art in which we've all become so accomplished - hypocrisy. You don't even have to antagonize or hurt your immediate family. On the contrary, knowing that no one knows all the answers, you respect them for their beliefs, remembering to maintain your mental distance to defend yourself against becoming a victim of another victim's coercion. Be your own person within yourself. It's alright to be a doubting Thomas. It's alright to mentally question someone else's "truths." In fact it's essential that you use this form of quality control, for doubt is the faltering beginning of mental emancipation.

Maturity is not something that happens at any given age. Maturity is something that grows. It is a burgeoning awareness that one is becoming less and less dependent on being programmed; not that we ever want to stop learning. Learning is a lifetime proposition. But, depending on the quality and truth of past programming, we can come to rely on our own judgement at a comparatively early age. It is the beginning of a preference for the wisdom of one's own judgement, one's own value system, rather than heeding car salesmen, following the loudest political exhibitionist, or believing in the damnation of the soul. On the other hand, self-reliance may not come until old age. In fact, it may never come.

The earlier a child can start thinking and questioning parental teachings, the sooner he will realize that a large component of parental love is the desire to perpetuate themselves in their children. Parental messages coerce the child to be like the parent: Be like me. Look like me. Do as I do. Think as I think. Believe as I believe. These teachings are more than messages of survival on a tried path; they are the unconscious manifestations of the desire for immortality. They are also the burdens and inhibitions of long dead generations. Without programming, the human mind is incapable of development. We all have minds that initially cry out for programming, for it is the foundation, essence and strength of our later human behavior. It is also the reason why most children become victims before the age of six.

Without verbalization, we can mentally repudiate, or put another's opinion on hold, without giving offense. When we are young, this is our only escape route. But an awareness that a truth is verifiable and cannot be reversed is our secret strength. On reaching the age of independent reason and behavior, a man treads his own path. One unalterable truth is that no one knows all the answers, for they involve a universe far beyond our ken - a world that might yet prove to have a superintelligence, and a devised pattern.

The simple message is that we must learn to take risks, to be independent and fly on our own wings; to be aware that it is our compliance, our insecurity, and our mental lethargy that allows others to manipulate us to actions that suit their own involuntary and mindless programming. We thus become the victims of victims. Victims of imaginative opinions. Victims of religious dogma. Victims of unscrupulous politicians. Victims of homosexuals, of child molesters, of war-mongers, of drug addicts, thieves, murderers, smokers, alcoholics, (or those who drink alcohol) or whatever. Long-term associations have more influence on our lives than those that are short-term, but the real problem is not who or what programs us to harmful behavior, so much as the fact that, without awareness of our vulnerability, we can easily become victims of another's programming.

However, to re-program ourselves to passive assessment over a lifetime of passive acceptance, with its accompanying thoughtless ritual and daily routine, is not easy. Only the very exceptional will recognize, and throw out the garbage in their lives in order to take control of a meaningful destiny. Self-determination is the rare achievement of the aware and very dedicated. An ongoing assertiveness with others must be tempered with consistent self-discipline and a vigilance in segregating truth from opinion. There will never be a time for completely relaxing the vigilance that maintains independent thought. There will always be an ongoing onslaught to bring the free-thinker on line with another victim's opinion, but the subsequent awareness of having independent freedom-of-thought will be a gradual awakening to a new and carefree day.